A SILVER THREAD

THE LYRIC POETRY *of*
CHARLES ANTHONY SILVESTRI

A SILVER THREAD

THE LYRIC POETRY *of* CHARLES ANTHONY SILVESTRI

WALTON MUSIC

GIA PUBLICATIONS, INC.

CHICAGO

Printed in the United States of America

Library of Congress Cataloging-in-Publication Data
Names: Silvestri, Charles Anthony, author.
Title: A silver thread : the lyric poetry of Charles Anthony Silvestri.
Description: Chicago : GIA Publications, Inc., [2019] | Includes indexes.
Identifiers: LCCN 2018057413 | ISBN 9781622773541 (paperback : alk. paper)
Subjects: LCSH: American poetry—21st century.
Classification: LCC PS3619.I55297 A6 2019 | DDC 811/.6—dc23
LC record available at https://lccn.loc.gov/2018057413

Silvestri, Charles Anthony, 1965–
   A Silver Thread.

ISBN 978-1-62277-354-1
G-9833

Cover art by John Burns
Design by Andrew Schultz
Edited by Susan LaBarr

Walton Music
A division of GIA Publications, Inc.
7404 S. Mason Ave.
Chicago, IL 60638

Distributed by GIA Publications, Inc.

www.waltonmusic.com

PREFACE

————◆▶————

When I was approached about creating this book, my first thoughts were, "There's not nearly enough material for a whole book," and "Why would anyone want a book of my poetry? I am not a poet!"

I have said many times that I am not a poet. I am a historian and an educator. All my training is in ancient and medieval history, not poetry. Although I have always appreciated beautiful word play and read a lot of poetry, I never wrote poems of my own. That's something for proper poets to do, artists who dedicate their education and work to the creation and teaching of poetry. I was not that person.

But now that I am confronted by the fact that here are nearly two hundred pages of poems that I wrote—most for composers for specific commissions, and a few just for me—I am forced to admit that maybe I *am* a poet after all, and maybe people *do* want to read my poetry. This is not easy for me to admit. I hide behind the label of "lyricist" rather than "poet." What I write is lyric poetry—words crafted explicitly to be sung. This genre is different, I think, from a poem to be read off the page. It's a poem, like any other, but one which requires attention to vowel sound, lilt and cadence, and a special sensitivity to the choral art. My job is always to give to composers exactly what they need to create an effective setting.

A SILVER THREAD

I am a very lucky poet, really. A poem is a powerful thing—it can touch the heart in ways that mere words cannot. But a lyric poem has the benefit of a custom soundtrack, so listeners get to experience my words with the added emotional power of music. The choral art is a magical synergy: the poet's heart, borne aloft by the genius of the composer's music, expertly interpreted by the director, internalized and brought to life by the singers, and then carried as a gift into the spirit of the listener. When it all works like it's supposed to, it is wondrous.

These lyric poems are presented roughly in the order in which I wrote them, to let my words flow to you as they flowed from me, beginning with that first flurry of texts I wrote for my friend Eric Whitacre in 2001. Had Eric been an accountant or engineer or barista instead of a composer, I would never have written those first words, from which sprung so many others. He asked me to translate a small poem into Latin, creating *Lux Aurumque*; and thus a whole career of writing for choral composers began. But it did not begin right away.

The years from 2001 to 2007 were very difficult. My wife, Julie, began to experience back pain, which turned out to be an aggressive attack of ovarian cancer. She fought heroically, but died in 2005, and I was left with two small children to raise alone. But with help we managed, and I am grateful to say we thrived. In those tough years I wrote very little, least of all anything to begin to process what we'd suffered, and what it all means. But during this period of grief the texts I wrote for Eric were performed often, and other composers began to contact me. In time the words came again, and I was asked to write more and more frequently, across the whole range of the human experience, for an ever-growing group of trusting composers. The process has been elemental in my rediscovery of the world after the long fog of grief and pain lifted. My texts have begun to show more and more personal reflection, as I have begun to find my voice. And I have only started to explore the deepest mysteries of love and death and reflect upon the whole sum of my experiences, thoughts, and feelings. I am honored that Walton and GIA thought my poetry worthy of a book of its own, and humbled that you chose to take a look through this journey of mine. There's more to come...

C.A.S.
Lawrence, Kansas
August, 2018

In 1999 I was commissioned to write a setting of Robert Frost's iconic poem *Stopping by Woods on a Snowy Evening*. I wrote the piece, premiered it, and moved forward with the publishing process, only to be unexpectedly denied permission from the Robert Frost estate. Devastated, I turned to poet Charles Anthony Silvestri, hoping for a miracle.

I asked Tony (as he is known to his friends) to do the impossible: replace *Stopping by Woods on a Snowy Evening* with an original poem of his own. It needed to be written with the exact metrical structure of the Frost; it needed to poetically "paint" musical gestures to match the music I had already written; and because *Stopping by Woods* famously ends with the line "and miles to go before I sleep", I needed Tony's poem to also end with the word "sleep." Truly a daunting task for any poet.

It took Tony less than a day to create a new work that surpassed even my wildest dreams—a simple, powerful poem called *Sleep*. Not only did his words perfectly flow with my existing music, his new poem was filled with all kinds of subtle poetic flourishes. He used the Shakespeare line "What dreams may come both dark and deep" as a hat tip to poets of the world, acknowledging the greatness of Robert Frost's original poem and looking back at the centuries-old tradition of poetry. Immediately following, Tony writes "Of flying wing and soaring leap," a reference to a piece we had just finished, *Leonardo Dreams of His Flying Machine*, looking forward. To my mind, Tony's poem gives *Sleep* an effervescence and depth that my original setting of *Stopping By Woods on a Snowy Evening* lacked, and unquestionably makes the music of *Sleep* far better than it should be.

I love the story of how *Sleep* came to be because it perfectly encapsulates the fluid nature of the way we work together. Tony and I have now collaborated on over a dozen works, trying every possible combination of the poet/composer collaboration. With *Leonardo Dreams of His Flying Machine* we worked almost like a songwriting team, sitting side by side at the piano, furiously writing lyrics and music at the same time. *Her Sacred Spirit Soars* was written in a more traditional way, with Tony completing the poem before I wrote a note of music. (Not to be missed: *Her Sacred Spirit Soars* is a formal Shakespearian sonnet, an ode to Queen Elizabeth I, complete with a clever acrostic, the first letter of each line spelling out HAIL FAIR ORIANA!).

Tony draws on his vast knowledge of many subjects to inform each new piece—subjects as disparate as history, science, religion, pop culture, politics—and then infuses the words with a razor-sharp intellect. And because he is a fine singer (he has a sweet, pure tenor voice) Tony also understands how to write truly singable lyrics: good vowels in the right places, phrases that roll easily off the tongue, and words that are true gifts to the composer, already bursting with their own internal music. Any honest vocal composer will tell you that the poet really does most of the heavy lifting; if the poem is good, the music almost writes itself.

Tony has been my best friend for over a quarter of a century, ever since we first sang together in college choir, and after all that time, after all these collaborations together, I feel I can safely say that Tony's personal life and his artistic life are driven by the same simple, guiding principle: service. Service to the music, service to the art of collaboration, service to humanity, service to beauty, service to truth. As a poet he is endlessly flexible, generous, gentle, creative, brilliant, dedicated, steadfast. As a man he is exactly the same. In fact, his poetry is not just a reflection of who he is as a person. It is a manifestation of his innermost character and ethos.

Eric Whitacre
November, 2018

CONTENTS
IN
CHRONOLOGICAL ORDER

CONTENTS

CONTENTS

CONTENTS

CONTENTS

SLEEP
2001 for Eric Whitacre

The evening hangs beneath the moon,
A silver thread on darkened dune.
With closing eyes and resting head
I know that sleep is coming soon.

Upon my pillow, safe in bed,
A thousand pictures fill my head.
I cannot sleep, my mind's a flight;
And yet my limbs seem made of lead.

If there are noises in the night,
A frightening shadow, flickering light…
Then I surrender unto sleep,
Where clouds of dream give second sight,

What dreams may come, both dark and deep,
Of flying wings and soaring leap,
As I surrender unto sleep,
As I surrender unto sleep.

A SILVER THREAD

LUX AURUMQUE
2001 for Eric Whitacre

Lux,
calida gravisque
pura velut aurum,
et canunt angeli
molliter modo natum.

LIGHT AND GOLD
LUX AURUMQUE
2001 for Eric Whitacre

Light,
warm and heavy
as pure gold,
and the angels sing softly
to the newborn babe.

(English poem by Edward Esch)

A SILVER THREAD

LEONARDO DREAMS
OF HIS FLYING MACHINE
2001 for Eric Whitacre
Italian fragments taken from the notebooks
of Leonardo Da Vinci

Leonardo Dreams of his Flying Machine.
Tormented by visions of flight and falling,
More wondrous and terrible each than the last,
Master Leonardo imagines an engine
To carry a man up into the sun...
And as he's dreaming the heavens call him,
softly whispering their siren-song:
"Leonardo. Leonardo, vieni á volare."
  ("Leonardo. Leonardo, come fly.")
L'uomo colle sua congiegniate e grandi ale,
  (A man with wings large enough, duly connected)
facciendo forza contro alla resistente aria.
  (might learn to overcome the resistance of the air.)

As the candles burn low he paces and writes,
Releasing purchased pigeons one by one
Into the golden Tuscan sunrise...
And as he dreams, again the calling,
The very air itself gives voice:
"Leonardo. Leonardo, vieni á volare".
  ("Leonardo. Leonardo, come fly.")

Vicina all'elemento del fuoco...
       (Close to the sphere of elemental fire...)
Scratching quill on crumpled paper,
Rete, canna, filo, carta.   (Net, cane, thread, paper.)
Images of wing and frame and fabric fastened tightly.
...sulla suprema sottile aria.
       (...in the highest and rarest atmosphere.)

As the midnight watchtower tolls,
Over rooftop, street and dome,
The triumph of a human being ascending
In the dreaming of a mortal man.
Leonardo steels himself,
takes one last breath,
and leaps...
"Leonardo, Vieni á Volare! Leonardo, Sognare!"
       ("Leonardo, come fly! Leonardo, Dream!")

A SILVER THREAD

HER SACRED SPIRIT SOARS
2001 for Eric Whitacre

Her sacred spirit soars o'er gilded spires,
 And breathes into creative fires a force;
  In well-tuned chants and chords of countless choirs
   Lives ever her immortal shadowed source.
From age to age the roll of poets grows;
 And yet, a lonely few are laurel-crowned,
  In whose sweet words her inspiration shows,
   Revealing insights deep and thoughts profound.
O shall Cecelia, or shall Goddess Muse
 Reach then to me across eternal skies?
  Is heaven's quick'ning fire but a ruse,
   Abiding rather here before mine eyes?
    Nearer than I dream'd is She whose fame
    All poets sing, whose glory all proclaim:
"LONG LIVE FAIR ORIANA!"

IN THE NAME OF GOD
2001

What does it matter?
Te Deum laudamus.
Baruch Atah Adonai, Eloheinu Melech Ha'Olam
Om na shivaim
Allahu Akbar!
Praise God from whom all blessings flow.
AUM
Kyrie eleison; Christe eleison; Kyrie eleison.
Hail Amida Buddha!
Hail to the Lotus Sutra of the Wonderful Law!
Hail Mary, full of grace!
Hare Krishna hare Krishna; Krishna Krishna hare hare!
La ilaha illallah muhammadur rasulullah.
The Lord is my Shepherd; I shall not want.
I am the Way and the Truth and the Life.
Om mani padme hum
Euouae!
Lord, make me an instrument of thy peace.
What is the sound of one hand clapping?
Know thyself.
Amen. Alleluia.

A SILVER THREAD

We trust in thee, O heavenly Father.
This we know: the earth does not belong to man;
    man belongs to the earth.
Bismillah al-Rahman, al-Rahim!
Hosanna in excelsis!
What difference does it make?
In nomine Patris, et Filii, et Spiritui Sancti.
The Tao that can be told of is not the eternal Tao;
The name that can be named is not the eternal name.
What does it matter?

IX SIMPLE PRAYERS
2002

I

For the Smallest Things, I thank you, God!
For buzzing bugs and baby birds newly-hatched;
For all that we cannot even see,
    whole worlds invisible right before our eyes;
For atoms and the even smaller particles,
And your living Force which binds them
    and all things together.
May we see, even in the Smallest Things,
    your attention and design.
Amen.

II

For the Dreaming, I thank you, God!
For its quiet, shimmering, unexpected beauty,
Its pretended truth and restless rest.
May I wake, and understand!
Amen.

III

For the Seasons of the Earth, I thank you, God!
For Summer's fruits, and Autumn's sparkling air;
For Winter's bitter chill and Spring's promised reward!
May we see in every Circle your simple infinity.
Amen.

A SILVER THREAD

IV
For the deep and undulating Sea, I thank you, God!
All who voyage, all who go in ships,
May they cross the majestic
    and unfathomable safely home again;
And may those who slip below find peace
Within the womb of our most dark and ancient Mother.
Amen.

V
For Love, I thank you, God!
For the feeling which no words can describe;
For the exquisite pain of the heart;
For the completion of one in another,
Two together in your Image.
May all be brought to Love,
    and all who love drink deeply!
Amen.

VI
For the most precious of gifts, our Children,
    I thank you, God!
May they grow up to be men and women of Light!
Amen.

VII
For the still, soft Silences, I thank you, God!
(Amen)

VIII
For Imagination, I thank you, God!
May we never tire of the One Great Story!
Amen.

IX
For the whole Universe, I thank you, God!
For twinkling Stars which dance their stately circles
        about the rotunda of the Heavens;
For its many-colored wonders -
        blue-white ice-tailed comets,
        ringed planets spinning,
        and irridescent nebulae burst from exploding stars!
All who turn their eyes up to the sky at night,
May they marvel at your great and intimate Creation!
Amen.

A SILVER THREAD

PARIS EN AVRIL
2002

Mon cher, je suis toujours
Enchantée d'amour,
Comme je suis de Paris en avril.

Quand je t'aperçois mon cœur veut sauter;
Après notre adieu je suis accablée.

Quand nous nous parlons
C'est comme la chanson
Des oiseaux dans un rêve gentil.

Soyons ensemble toujours, mon amour,
Du moins jusqu'à Paris en avril.

APRIL IN PARIS
PARIS EN AVRIL
2002

My dear, I am always
Enchanted by love,
Just as I am by April in Paris.

When I see you my heart wants to jump;
After our goodbye I am desolated.

When we speak to one another
It is like the song of birds
In a gentle dream.

May we always be together, my love,
At least until Paris in April.

A SILVER THREAD

DAY IS DONE
2003

Day is done, but love unfailing
Dwells ever here;
Shadows fall, but hope, prevailing,
Calms every fear.
God, our Maker, none forsaking,
Take our hearts, of Love's own making,
Watch our sleeping, guard our waking,
Be always near.

Dark descends, but light unending
Shines through our night;
You are with us, ever lending
New strength to sight:
One in love, your truth confessing,
One in hope of heaven's blessing,
May we see, in love's possessing,
Love's endless light!

Eyes will close, but you unsleeping
Watch by our side;
Death may come, in love's safe keeping
Still we abide.
God of love, all evil quelling,
Sin forgiving, fear dispelling,
Stay with us, our hearts indwelling,
This eventide.

INVESTITURE OF SIR ADAM
2003

The King he spoke unto his newly vested Knight, saying:

"Accept these your shield and standard, as symbols of
	your name and family.
Let them be an inspiration to you, and a herald to others.
May men of virtue who see them have hope,
	and the wicked despair.

"Wear these your spurs, to goad you on your way.
The road to the future is often hard, and even the mighty
	falter who are not thus equipped.
May they lead you to your destiny.

"Wield this your sword, forged in flame, a mighty steel,
Fit indeed for a Knight of your exception and integrity.
Name it well; and may it ever come twixt you and Death's
	dark victory.

"Rise, Sir, take these gifts, and mark you use them wisely.
For the good of this House
	and this Kingdom depend on you,
Our hero, our second son, and our salvation."

And the Knight replied:

"Ever shall I live even as you command, dread King.
My arms, my honor, my very life are in your service."

A SILVER THREAD

PSALM 91
2003 for Dale Jergenson

All you who dwell in the shelter of God
      and anthems of refuge sing,
Our God shall deliver from danger's snare,
      and shield beneath His mighty wing.

You shall not be afraid of the terrors of night,
      nor the arrows that fly by day;
Though foes may surround you, and dark closes in,
      the Lord He will keep them at bay.

Because you have made a great God your own refuge,
      the Almighty your dwelling-place,
The forces of evil cannot touch you there,
      protected by His loving grace.

For His angels will guard your every step,
      and keep you in all of your ways;
And if you should falter they'll bear you up,
      watching over you all of your days.

THE PACIFIC
2006 for Costas Dafnis

I. Sunrise

The sun will come.
But now, only the sound of the waves,
Gently lapping;
Like the shallow breath of a sleeping giant.
The sun will come.
It will come and illuminate the vast expanses,
As black loses black and becomes violet.
The sun will come from behind the cliff,
Like a friend back from a long night's journey,
Bringing gifts of gray and white and gold.

II. The Deep

How calm you look today—
But I know what you hide.
Beneath your glassy canopy,
Under your dance of gentle swells and playful spray,
Churns a teeming storm of life and death.
What secrets yet dwell deep in your womb,
O most dark and ancient Mother?

A SILVER THREAD

III. Sunset

The shadows turn and lengthen
Behind the slender palms,
Which stand like swaying sentinels
Before a silver road,

Beyond whose gates are foamy whispers
Calling me
To join their ever-turning dance
Of surf, and tide, and day, and season.

Where will you take me, O Silver Road?
Toward new day, new life, new home
Across the sea?
Across the sea,
Into that rugged range of cloudscape
Slowly exploding
Pink, and white, and burnished gold.

OREAD FAREWELL
2007 for Dan Forrest

The time has come to say farewell;
And though my heart be heavy,
I promise still to remember ye
E'en though we say, "Farewell."

The flow'rs that bloom'd in Summer's sun
Have lost their fleeting glory,
And all but died in Winter's chill;
And we must say, "Farewell."

So brief a time has come and gone
Since first we sang together;
But bittersweet is that music now
That we must say, "Farewell."

Now we must part, and fare ye well
In all that ye endeavor!
And last, I pray—fondly think of me,
Whene'er you say, "Farewell."

A SILVER THREAD

ROSA MORIENDA
2007

Rosa tempus conteret suaviter florescere,
Ita sua varia occultissima patescere;
Simul eam incipis subtiliter cognoscere…
Moritur.

THE DYING ROSE
ROSA MORIENDA
2007

The Rose takes her sweet time to open up,
thus to reveal her manifold mysteries;
and just when you begin to understand her...
she dies.

A SILVER THREAD

THE CANTICLE OF JOSEPH
2008

The ancient prophets long foretold
The coming of this hour:
A rising star,
A humble birth
In the city of David, my father.
O promised Messiah, Holy Child!

My virgin wife is delivered of her spirit-son;
This girl, whom I accepted
Out of duty to the Lord,
Has honored me with a son in my old age,
And a place in the history of Israel.
O blessed Maid and Mother!

And so the time has come
To be a father once again.
But what kind of father can I be
To this Son, who is not my son?
What can I teach Him who has come to Teach?
O Immanuel, God With Us!

I can only show the wooden way,
The way of flesh and blood.
He will learn to mill and carve and plane and sand,
To fit the mortise with the tenon,
To brace with cross and nail.
O Beginning, and O End!

I will teach him the ways our people
Honor the Lord, our God:
Through study, teaching and sacrifice;
To prepare his Heart, his Body, and his Brow
For the sacred work he comes to accomplish.
O Child, O Shepherd, O King!

A SILVER THREAD

'TIS SEVEN DAYS
2008

'Tis seven days since I have seen my love,
And seven silver daggers pierce my heart;
And yet my love for her is strong enough
For seven times a thousand days apart.
My lady's gone away from me—with him—
To play her part: the Lady to his Knight;
And I am left alone, bereft, and grim,
With nothing for a fortnight but to write.
And so, I write; in writing keep her close.
The pen (my fingertip) a mischief makes;
The velvet vellum skin (her soft repose)
My letters tickle, teasing, and she shakes.
Her husband knoweth not, and never will—
I ravish her, and take her with my quill.

WHEN GENTLE BREEZES BLOW
2008

When gentle breezes blow across the grass
And white wheat waves like undulating sea,
Like memory he comes, a breath, to pass
Through cheerful chime and dance with rustling tree.
The engine of the sail, the lift of flight,
Can in an instant alter from a friend
To howling tempest, sandstorm blinding sight
And sense until tornado's vicious end.
What is the Wind? And whither? Whence? And why?
Unseen he's journeyed, without rest or sleep,
His endless circling route 'cross global sky
Since first He breathed across the darkened deep.
The Breath of God is He, of Will the rush,
His whisper, of the still, small voice the hush.

A SILVER THREAD

HEAVEN UNFOLDING
2009 for Andrea Ramsey

Heaven is here unfolding,
Where starlight and wonder mingle,
Where sky and earth collide
In the vast expanses of the universe
And in the smallest interstitial spaces of cell and atom.

In quiet moments, in soaring songs of light,
In unexpected beauty, in a smile,
In laughter and in love, in harmony and hope,
In the depths of solitude
As in the joy of fellowship;

In the burnished golden light of Autumn,
In Death, and in sweet partings;
Just as in the quickening fire of newfound love,
Is Heaven here unfolding.

Drink deeply!
For widely flows the fountain,
And deep is Heaven here on earth.

ACROSS THE VAST, ETERNAL SKY
2010 for Ola Gjeilo

Weary, I fly,
Across the vast eternal sky,
High in the heavens,
Where awaits my destiny.

Grey skies are thickening;
Soon now my time will come,
Time to return home
'Cross the vast eternal sky.

When I was young I flew in the velvet night;
Shining by day, a firebird bathed in light!
Grey now my feathers, which once were red and gold;
My destiny to soar up to the sun!

Sunlight shines on my face;
This is my grace, to be
Restored, born again,
In flame!

Do not despair that I am gone away;
I will appear again
When the sunset paints
Flames across the vast eternal sky!

A CHRISTMAS LULLABY
2010 for Dan Forrest

Lullaby, Lullaby,
Rest now my sweeting,
Oh my Child, close your eyes!
Angel voices softly singing
Carols for their newborn King.
Lullaby, Lullaby,
Whisper and sigh,
Lullaby, Lullaby, Lullaby.

Lullaby, Lullaby,
Silently waiting,
All creation greets the Child;
Holy Child, fulfill our longing,
Our foretold salvation bring.
Lullaby, Lullaby,
Whisper and sigh,
Lullaby, Lullaby, Lullaby.

I RISE!
2010 for Ola Gjeilo

I rise!
And in my rising,
I sing the coming of the King!
Banished are my doubts and fears,
Like great storm-clouds dawn-scattered;
Arise! Rise up O King divine,
And speak to me a wisdom
That only You can fathom,
My inner Self, my Soul, my King,
Arising deep within my heart.
The Cosmic Wanderer
Returns from Within
At this, the Dawn of Grace.

A SILVER THREAD

NOX AURUMQUE
2010 for Eric Whitacre

Aurum,
Infuscatum et obscurum,
Canens noctis,
Canens mortis,
Acquiescens canendo…

Et angelum somnit aurorarum et bellorum,
Saeculorum aurorum fundit lacrimas,
Lacrimas rerum bellorum.

O arma!
O lamina aurata!
Gestu graves nimium,
Graves nimium volatu.

Aurum,
Infuscatum et torpidum
Suscita!
Dilabere ex armis in alam!
Volemus iterum,
Alte supra murum;
Angeli renascentes et exultantes ad alas
Aurorarum, Aurorum, Somniorum.

Aurum,
Canens alarum,
Canens umbrarum.

NIGHT AND GOLD
NOX AURUMQUE
2010 for Eric Whitacre

Gold,
Tarnished and dark,
Singing of night,
Singing of death,
Singing itself to sleep…

And an angel dreams of dawnings, and of war.
She weeps tears of the golden times,
Tears of the cost of war.

O shield!
O gilded blade!
You are too heavy to carry
Too heavy for flight.

Gold,
Tarnished and weary,
Awaken!
Melt from weapon into wing!
Let us soar again,
High above this wall;
Angels reborn and rejoicing
With wings made
Of Dawn, of Gold,
Of Dream.

Gold,
Singing of wings,
Singing of shadows…

A SILVER THREAD

INTO THE MORNING
2010 for Ola Gjeilo

Darkness is a sacred cloak
Enveloping the soul
As it does the earth,
In spacious, velvet night;
And the spark within
Remains eternal, true,
An assurance of the Joy
Forever borne by dark
Into the morning.

OVER HAVET – ACROSS THE SEA
2010 for Dan Forrest

My eyes look out,
Grey as the grey North-Sky,
Across the sea,
The sea of hope and opportunity.
The wander-lust of my people wells up,
Calling me to go—

Across the sea,	*Over havet,*
Across the sea,	*Over havet,*
Across the beckoning sea.	*Over det lokkende havet.*

In this great ship-belly I wait,
With others like me
Set out to make a better life.
And now we stand together, line by line,
Masses huddled in the shadow of Liberty.
We've come so far

Across the sea,	*Over havet,*
Across the sea,	*Over havet,*
Across the storm-tossed sea.	*Over det stormfulle havet.*

A SILVER THREAD

Work is hard in this New World,
As hard as in the Old;
But this land I work is soon to be my own—
A farm, a house, a wife, a child—
Fields of grain stretched out before me;
My home
Across the sea,   *Over havet,*
Across the sea,   *Over havet,*
Across the amber sea.   *Over det ravgule havet.*

My eyes look out,
Grey as my grey hair now,
Across the sea,
From poverty and possibility
To the richest blessings a man can ever know,
Thankful now as I go,
Across the sea,   *Over havet,*
Across the sea,   *Over havet,*
Across the eternal sea.   *Over det evige havet.*

TUNDRA
2010 for Ola Gjeilo

Wide, worn and weathered,
Sacred expanse
Of green and white and granite grey;
Snowy patches strewn,
Anchored to the craggy earth,
Unmoving;
While clouds dance
Across the vast, eternal sky.

A SILVER THREAD

THE NOVICE
2011

I
The Novice sits in the cold Scriptorium,
Cat curled at his feet,
Leaves laid out before him,
Ready for illumination.
Minium, vermilion,
Ochre, malachite,
Vine black, lead white,
Gold and lapis lazuli,
Gifts from far across the sea—
Of earth and of dark alchemy.

His clever marginalia are more than merely that:
Ivy and acanthus turning,
Decoration, illumination,
Awakening the sleepy words.

And as he paints, he hums the antiphon,
Adveni, Sapientia, donum invernalis…
    (Come, Wisdom, gift of winter…)

II
The bell tolls the Vesper hour.
Dark comes early now.
The cat sleeps still,
Indifferent to the Hours,
Or the season.

The Novice loves this time of waiting.
As cold comes, and cruel winds howl,
Inside his heart a fire glows,
The fire of Wisdom,
The fire of Memory,
The fire of Patience
For the Long-Awaited.

As he closes the Scriptorium
The Novice sings the daily antiphon,
So common, and so rare,
Like the voice of an old friend
Who visits only once a year.
Adveni, Sapientia, donum invernalis…

III
Shadows lengthen across the cloister,
His brothers, in procession paired,
Toward the Chapel doors,
Wooly bundled against the bracing cold.

The Novice takes his place in line,
With an inward smile
Unbecoming the cold solemnity;
For he knows this night,
And when his heart sings,
He sings to Her.
Adveni, Sapientia, donum invernalis…

A SILVER THREAD

ADVENI, SAPIENTIA
2011

Adveni, sapientia,
Donum invernalis—
Confirma nos vigilare
Ad quem adventurum.

Adveni, nix benefica,
Cadens de altissimo—
Vela terram dormientem
Candido purissimo.

Adveni, nox longissima,
Gemina aestatis—
Admone nos gaudium
Mane advenire.

Adveni, flamma antiqua,
Potens et arcana—
Focos nobis excita
Et cordes nobis sana.

Adveni, sancta domina,
Regina invernalis—
Renova nos etiam
Dum annum circumages.

Adveni, lucis animus,
Natus aeternalis—
Omnia reficere
Fraterculus beatus.

COME THOU, WISDOM
ADVENI, SAPIENTIA
2011

Come thou, Wisdom,
Gift of Winter—
Strengthen us to wait
For that which is to come.

Come thou, Healing Snow,
Falling from the highest height—
Blanket the sleeping earth
In purest white.

Come thou, Longest Night,
Summer's twin—
Remind us that joy
Comes in the morning.

Come thou, Ancient Flame,
Powerful and secret—
Kindle our hearths
And mend our hearts.

Come thou, Holy Lady,
Queen of Winter—
Renew us
Even as you turn the year.

Come thou, Spirit of Light,
Eternally born
To make all things new—
Blessed little brother.

A SILVER THREAD

THE CHELSEA CAROL
2011 for Eric Whitacre

Adveni, sapientia,
Donum hinvernale—
Confirma nos vigilantes
Ad quem adventurum.

Adveni, adveni somnifera,
Aevifera,
Regina solis siderum.

Adveni, adveni lunifera,
Glacifera,
Regina mater temporum.

Sancta domina regina!
Sancta domina argentea!
Sancta domina purissima!

Adveni, adveni florifera,
Solifera,
Regina lucis candida.

Adveni, adveni messifera,
Nivifera,
Regina Somnis Magistra!

Adveni, mater!
Adveni ad nos!
Adveni, domina!

THE CHELSEA CAROL
2011 for Eric Whitacre

Come thou, Wisdom,
Gift of Winter—
Strengthen us to wait
For him who is to come.

Come thou, come dream-bearer,
Time-bearer,
Queen of sun and stars.

Come thou, come moon-bearer,
Frost-bearer,
Queen and mother of the seasons.

Holy lady, Queen!
Holy lady of silver!
Purest holy lady!

Come thou, come flower-bearer,
Sun bearer,
Queen of gleaming white light.

Come thou, come sheaf-bearer,
Snow bearer,
Queen, Mistress of Dreams.

Come, Thou, Mother!
Come to us!
Come Lady!

A SILVER THREAD

FAITH, LOVE, BEAUTY, HOPE
2011 for Tobias Forster

I. FAITH

Faith is a rock, a mighty fortress,
A pathway to grace and a loving God.
Faith is unchanging, simple, eternal—
"The Way and the Truth," saith the Lord.

But others say that God is an illusion—
That science is the only way;
Fixed, eternal Laws of Nature
Over space and time hold sway.

Wiser ones have an elemental Faith,
An altar of contradiction;
The universe is a complicated place,
Not fixed, not ever simple.

For God resides in the infinite expanse,
Both the cosmic and the quantum,
Revealed in pattern and in wonder—
Equal halves of one true Faith.

II. LOVE and BEAUTY

Beauty is spread out all around us;
But we do not see it.
From home to work and back again
We travel to and fro,
As in a sort of lonely dream
From which we choose not to wake.

Along our way the flowers bloom,
Their duty they fulfill
As we rush by, oblivious,
Carrying our cares.
Their beauty blooms and dies unnoticed—
A sin of ignorance.

And Love, that most sublime expression
Of all that is Divine,
We're loath to risk, or we take for granted,
Or we dilute its power,
Confusing Love with Like or Want,
Equating it with Desire.

Through Love we become our higher selves,
The fullness of our being;
In giving of the Self to Other
We do not lose, but gain—
Awakened from our lonely dream,
Life's Beauty we attain.

A SILVER THREAD

III. HOPE

Hope is a river ever-flowing,
Born from the very Firmament;
Source of fulfillment,
Life-everlasting,
Deep understanding, seed of Peace.

Hope is the source of inspiration,
Fountain of all creative fire;
Leading me onward
Toward the horizon
Singing a vision from within.

Hope is a light in times of darkness,
Healing and balm for all my pain;
Solace and comfort
Hope for tomorrow,
Teaching my heart to love again.

So ever onward flows my journey,
Fortified by these virtues three:
Faith elemental,
Love eternal,
Hope in a future clear and bright.

LIGHT, LOVE
2011 for Alwin Schronen

Just as the purest, whitest light can part,
Refract in prismic crystal facets clear
And splendid shatter into spectrum hues
Enough indeed to color all our art;

And just as shining stars, their inner grace
And flashing fire completely spent, explode,
Great glowing clouds of color-splashes smear
Across the black expanse of endless space;

So do our light, our fire, our graces move,
From our intention outward emanate,
Refracting through the prisms of our soul:
Our hearts, our hands, our voices, and our love.

THE RAKE
2011 for John Armstrong

There once was a boy, and he captured my heart;
He was handsome and charming, romantic and
smart.
He whispered to me that he's done with the sea,
And he promised as we kissed we never would part.

But he sailed away.
He promised me he would stay!
I gave my innocence and gave my love,
And if he returns to me he will pay!
Some day…

"My lady, I swoon, my passions ablaze,
I will love you, adore you, for all of my days…"
And he loves them all in each port-of-call
The Annabelles, the Sarahs, the Lucys, the Mays,

Then he sails away.
He promises he will stay.
He takes their innocence, enjoys their love,
Expecting never, ever to pay,
One day…

He returned one day.
She promised herself he would pay;
But he was penitent and pledged his love,
And promised that he'd never sail away
One day…
Some day…
Sail away…

A SILVER THREAD

A RIVER'S LAMENT
2011 for Elena Kats-Chernin
        and the King's Singers

I
I am born where clouds descend
To kiss the mountain top

The sky is my father
The earth is my mother
I gather together
With fingers spread out
The waters that fall from
The storm and the thunder
With water that flows through
The caverns below

A trickle at the melting snow line
The golden sunlight flashes down
I dance along the the rocky creekbeds
As ever faster down I flow

One by one my fingers gather
Merging into wider streams
Waters drawn from every mountain
Mingled in a silver flow

Twisting, turning, serpentine,
I run through quiet, sacred groves
The ancient trees untouched and tall
All seem to whisper softly

I rush toward the sleeping valley
Carving canyon cliffs
Playing catch-me-if-you-can
Against the rising sun

Ever swifter now I hasten
Plunging down the granite cliff
Where mist and sun create a rainbow
Soaring high above the falls

My swift cold current
And warmer eddies still
Are home and life to all creation:

Dancing otter, digging wombat
Buzzing insect, wading bird
All come to me

For I am Water
I am the Glassway
For I am the Life-Bearer
I am a River
Wide and Mighty!

A SILVER THREAD

II
Steamer bells are ringing
Breaking in the silence
Sooty smoke is rising
Covering the dawn

Clacky paddle steamers
Froth the busy waters
As they daily jostle
Barging heavy goods

Up and down the teeming valley
Industry and trade
From the spreading delta
Toward the falls

Singing stevedores on busy quays
Heave the crates and bales and load the barrels

Laughing children play along the muddy banks
Skipping stones break the glassy surface of the water

Hand in hand young lovers stroll
Beside the mill wheel ever-turning
Among the wild flowers

I am He...
He Who Flows...
River...
Mighty...

Up and down the valley
Teeming up and down
Spreading from the delta
To the Falls

Up and down the valley
Bustling down they spread
Industry and trade
Above the falls

I am ever-carrying
I am ever-flowing
From the delta to the falls
Ever more extending
I am...

A SILVER THREAD

III
I am diminished…

Snowmelt streams no longer gather
At the granite falls

The lake is low now
Water retreating
Revealing rocks turned white
Beneath the scorching sun

I am diminished…

Fish are few
The wombats gone
The eyes of men grow deep

I am diminished…

On the muddy banks
The grasses wither
Parched and dead

I am diminished…
All is still across the valley

I'm still a River
Wide and mighty
Flowing through stone
In caverns below

All is still…

I am diminished…

IV
Storm clouds billowing
Heaven opens, and rain returns
Sacred water
Resurrection,
Healing balm
Kiss the mountaintop
Flow of water
Flow of time
Ever flowing, I awaken
Splashing, dancing
I am born again
Skipping, rushing over the falls

Flowing through the valley
Healing rain returns
Rushing to the delta
Much has changed

A SILVER THREAD

The rain returns
Beckoning otter and bird
Insects and mammals return
Leaping over granite falls
Bringing life to the world

Hand in hand they stroll
Everything has changed
Nothing is the same
Beside the Old Mill Inn
I remember mill wheel turning
Painters try to capture my meander

Steamer now is still
Everything has changed
Nothing is the same
Casino on the Quays
Shoppers bustle
Where once were crates and barrels

When the rain returns
I am born again
Although much has changed
Yet I still remain

I am a river, wide and mighty
Twisting and turning, flowing through time
I am a river, son of the earth and sky
I am a river, wide and mighty,
Twisting and turning, flowing through time
I am a river, flowing through eternity
I am a river and I flow forever
I know where I'm going and always arrive at the sea
That which you do to me you also do to yourself
Ancient and elemental is my power
I am the thread that binds the sky to the earth
I am the thread that binds the earth to the sea
I am the thread that binds all creation
I am a river endlessly flowing
I am the bringer of life to the valley
I am a river wide and mighty...

A SILVER THREAD

UTRUMNE EST ORNATUM
2011 for Sidney Sussex College, Cambridge

In parietes, lapides,
In stabula caelata
Perfundebamus lacrimas,
Et gaudia oblata.

Munera nostra gratiae
Diu aggregabantur;
Thesauri ipsi idola
Ne quando venerentur.

Auratas turres spolia,
Evelle pavimentum—
Permanet numen Domini
Utrumne est ornatum.

DECORATED OR NOT
UTRUMNE EST ORNATUM
2011 for Sidney Sussex College, Cambridge

Into these walls, these stones,
These carved choir stalls
We have poured our tears
And joys, as offerings.

Our gifts of thanks
Have long gathered;
May these same treasures
Never themselves become idols.

Tear down the gilded spires,
Rip up the fancy floor—
The spirit of God remains,
Even without the trappings.

A SILVER THREAD

THE SEASONS OF MY HEART
2011

When Summer's sun is shining bright,
And spreads the earth with golden light,
The days grow long, the shadows tall,
The smell of jasmine fills the night.

When Autumn leaves begin to fall,
And pile against the garden wall,
Begin new colors to appear—
An umber, gold and crimson pall.

And when the Winter's coming near,
With bitter cold and darkness, fear
Fear not! The Spring will yet restart
The turning circle of the year.

Whatever season plays its part,
My love for you shall not depart;
You are my love, my life, my joy,
Through all the seasons of my heart.

VOCES LUCIS
2011 for Andrea Ramsey

Voces lucis
Molliter in nocte
Sussurantes mihi
Cum lassus sum;

Voces lucis,
Quid memoratis?
Cantate et audiam,
Nam timeo.

"Non timeas,
Nam adsumus semper!
Circumdamus te,
Protegimus de malo.
Salvebunt onmia
Si fides nobis."

Voces lucis
Verba vestra audio
Timor meus fugit;
Paratus sum.

A SILVER THREAD

VOICES OF LIGHT
VOCES LUCIS
2011 for Andrea Ramsey

Voices of light,
Gently in the night,
Whispering to me
When I am weary.

Voices of light,
What are you telling me?
Sing, and I will listen,
For I am afraid.

"Do not be afraid,
For we are with you always!
We surround you,
Shield you from evil.
All shall be well
If you but trust in us!"

Voices of light,
My fear has fled;
I hear your words.
I am ready.

A BRONZE TRIPTYCH
2012 for Dan Forrest

I
I was born in deepest veins   *Nata sum in venas altissimas*
      of tin and copper cold—
The metal blood of mother earth
Mined, melted, mixed,
Forged in fire,
Wrought by arms into arms
Sword and shield and spear!   *Gladius, cetratus, hasta*
Cannon clash and clamor,   *Concursus, tormento*
Dealing Death!

II
But then I was reborn.
When now my bronze strikes bronze
'Tis not in clash of arms
Or blast of fire,
But to ring the vesper hour,
Or I may toll in requiem
As those who fall asleep
Are gathered back to earth.

A SILVER THREAD

III
And oh! To peal in celebration!
In victory, in festival,
In carillon of joy!
But greater still will be to sing
The dawning of that day
When war shall cease,
And on earth, peace
Everlasting I will ring!

DREAMWEAVER
2012 for Ola Gjeilo

Listen!
I sing the sacred vision
Of the All-Wise Wanderer,
The Weaver of Dreams.

On Christmas Eve he fell asleep,
So deep, so deep,
And woke upon Epiphany
With tales to tell.

He hurried to the holy Mass
And stood upon the threshold;
The warp and weft of wandering
He wove into his tale.

And this was his dreamsong:

My journey began
In a rugged land,
Hard and fast
And unforgiving.
I made my way.

A SILVER THREAD

Beasts there were,
And wilder things,
And shades of night
Were in that land;
I was afraid.

The monster's claws
Tore at my cloak;
With piercing eyes
They saw my soul.
I ran away.

For many leagues
I traveled west
Until at last—
My journey's end—
I saw the Bridge!

Stretching out
Across the sky,
The way was barred
To all but wise.
I went across.

This bridge was spanned   across a sea of ice—
A silver band,   a way to Paradise.
A fair wide land   did open up at last;
I stopped to stand   where Future reckons Past.

And in that place the Pilgrim Church did rise
Where, full of grace, our Holy Mother wise
Bade me embrace her heart of gold and red;
And o'er her face a loving smile was spread.

She spoke in gentle tone and bade me go
Where every sin is known, where north winds blow,
Unto the very throne of God to see
How sorrow is self-sown, forgiveness, free.

I met a man, whose cloak was stained in blood,
All mired was he, up to his knees in mud;
He held a frightened child under his arm,
And bitterly he wept for causing harm.

Another one there was, cloaked all in lead;
Behind her eyes the fire almost dead,
The weight worn heavy on her head—regret—
For past mistakes and those not present yet.

And many more I saw who were in pain—
Of loneliness, of fear, of loss or gain—
Attached, betrayed, obsessed, resigned, afraid,
Ensnared in traps, which they themselves had made.

Amid this gath'ring of the self-accursed
A mighty noise into the glooming burst:
A blast of trumpet, terrible to hear,
The harbinger of Judgment drawing near.

A SILVER THREAD

On midnight horse the great Deceiver came,
These thralls of his illusions for to claim.
The sinning souls like aspens trembling
Made hasty penance for their suffering.

And lo, there came another trumpet blast, like thunder echoing
in the heavens. From on high came St. Michael the
Defender, Protector of Souls, resplendent in gleaming armor.
The Captain of the Heavenly Host stood between Satan and
the sinning souls. Defender and Deceiver faced one-another,
until Michael raised aloft his flaming sword and sang the
battle-cry of old.

And with him appeared the Christ, wreathed in light, flanked
by saints and angels beyond number, and crowned as King
and Judge over all the earth. The Adversary turned in fear,
and fled from before the Glory of the Lord and the Host of
Heaven.

Among the souls
Who trembled there
Burdened down
With sin and fear,
I took my place.

To Christ the Judge
St. Michael spoke,
Defending us
Despite our shame.
I hung my head.

So one by one
We stood alone
Before our Maker
And our Judge.
He called my name.

His burning heart
Loved away my shame,
And forged my soul
Anew by Grace—
I was redeemed!

Listen!
I sing the sacred vision
Of the All-Wise Wanderer,
The Weaver of Dreams,
Who fell asleep,
So deep, so deep,
And woke with tales to tell,
A dreamsong woven for you.
So listen!

A SILVER THREAD

LUMINOUS NIGHT OF THE SOUL
2012 for Ola Gjeilo

Long before music was sung by a choir,
Long before silver was shaped in the fire,
Long before poets inspired the heart,
You were the Spirit of all that is art.

You give the potter the feel of the clay;
You give the actor the right part to play;
You give the author a story to tell;
You are the prayer in the sound of a bell.

Praise to all lovers who feel your desire!
Praise to all music which soars to inspire!
Praise to the wonders of Thy artistry
Our Divine Spirit, all glory to Thee.

TO SING
2012 for Tom Vignieri

When faced with many questions, trials, and doubt,
When choices loom before us, challenging,
We try to understand what life's about,
To know what paths to take, what words to sing.
We hear the many mentor voices call,
Reminding us to make all choices good.
We feel their reassurance when we fall,
Whenever we do other than we should.
So, nurtured thus, this sacred fire we bear.
Our quest: to learn, to journey, and to grow,
To make no little plans, to dream, to dare,
To sing our stories so that all can know:
This human life appears for such short space,
So LIVE, and make the world a better place.

A SILVER THREAD

VIRGO, MATER, REGINA
2012 for Costas Dafnis

I
Maria Virgo,
"Fiat mihi" tuum
Mundum transformavit;
O Maria,
Ancilla domini,
Virgo purissima,
Gratia plena—
Maria Virgo,
Ora pro nobis!

II
Maria Mater,
Nutribas nutritorem
Et docebas doctorem;
O Maria,
Mater fidelis,
Janua caeli,
Patrona amoris—
Maria Mater,
Ora pro nobis!

III
Maria Regina,
In caelo intercede
Pro nobis domini;
O Maria,
Regina pacis,
Domina sanctorum
Et angelorum—
Maria Regina,
Ora pro nobis!

A SILVER THREAD

VIRGIN, MOTHER, QUEEN
VIRGO, MATER, REGINA
2012 for Costas Dafnis

I
Maria Virgin,
Your "Let it be"
Transformed the world;
O Maria,
Handmaid of God,
Virgin most pure,
Full of grace—
Maria Virgin,
Pray for us!

II
Maria Mother,
You nurtured the Nurturer
And taught the Teacher;
O Maria,
Faithful mother,
Portal of Heaven,
Mistress of Love—
Maria Mother,
Pray for us!

III
Maria Queen,
Intercede for us
To the Lord in Heaven;
O Maria,
Queen of peace,
Lady of saints
And of angels—
Maria Queen,
Pray for us!

A SILVER THREAD

VOX AURUMQUE
2012 for Eric Whitacre

Vox aurumque
Clamor armaque
Tenebrae arcanaque
In campo proelii
Comiscentur

Et canunt angeli
Eruntne carmina bellica?
Eruntne alae et aurorae lucis?
Ululabimusne caedem?
Et volabimusne alis armatis?

Vox aurumque
Nex amorque
Lux umbraque
In acie terribili
Ordinantur
Et canunt angeli
Ferite!

Lux aurea coruscat
De pennis politis
De campitorum oculis
De gladiorum concursu
Chaos, clamor, caedes, chalybs
Confusio, caecitas, corruptio

Et canunt angeli
Qui veniet?
Qui nos ducet?
Qui erit vox nostra?

A SILVER THREAD

VOICE AND GOLD
VOX AURUMQUE
2012 for Eric Whitacre

Voice and gold
War cries and arms
Secrets and shadow
All are mingled
On the field of battle

And the angels sing
Will there be songs of war?
Will there be wings and dawns of light?
Will we shriek out slaughter?
And shall we fly with armored wings?

Voice and gold
Murder and love
Light and dark
Are arrayed
In dread battle line
And the angels sing
Attack!

Golden light glitters
From polished pinions
From the eyes of the war-steed
From the clash of swords
Chaos, clamor, slaughter, steel
Confusion, blindness, ruin

And the angels sing
Who will come?
Who will lead us?
Who will be our voice?

THE DIVINE WAVE
2013 for Dan Forrest

Rose and indigo
Mingle as the rising sun
Heralds a new day.
All is silence—from pebble
To heart of ancient mountain.

Ocean waves whisper
Secrets to the silent shore,
Sand and foam embrace.
The sea has many secrets
Beneath her veil of billows.

Without warning
The mountains tremble
And the sea rises up;
A wall of water
Sweeps away our future
In an instant.

All things fade away—
We are only wanderers
Upon this moment;
And yet we sing together,
In love against all shadows.

HIMENAMI   秘波
THE DIVINE WAVE
2013 for Dan Forrest

Ai-to Hi-ni	藍と緋に
Hama-wo someyuku	浜を染め行く
Akatsuki-no	暁の
Shizuka-ni nemuru	閑かに睡る
Yama-mo Koishi-mo	山も小石も
Sunahama-ni	砂浜に
Yosete-ha kaesu	寄せては返す
Himenami-ha	秘め波は
Chitabi sasayaku	千度囁く
Sono Himegoto-wo	その秘め事を
Niwaka-ni	俄かに
Yama furue	山震え
Umi-ha fukure	海は膨れ
Mizukabe-ga	水壁が
Mirai-no Hi-wo	未来の灯を
Oshinagasu	押し流す
Ushinaite	失いて
Ima konotoki-ha	今このときは
Samayoedo	彷徨えど
Warera utaou	我ら歌おう
Ai-wo Chikara-ni	愛をちからに

Japanese translation: Takako Helbig

A SILVER THREAD

BIG SKY
2013 for Ola Gjeilo

Golden sunlight gleams off the
Rugged peaks soar up into
Big sky spreads out like a
Blue embrace of you

Splashing streams tumble into
Rushing river cuts through
Pine tree valley full of
Green memories of you

    Every time I see that great big sky I
    Think of you and wonder why?
    I can almost feel you right here with me
    Every time I see that great big sky!

Eagles soar high above the
Misty pine-tops that grow
Roots go deep in the big earth
Deep as my love for you

SAINTE-CHAPELLE
2013 for Eric Whitacre

Castissima virgo
Advenit in capellam;
Et angeli in vitro
Molliter cantaverunt,

"Hosanna in excelsis!"

Illa castissima
Susurravit,

"Sanctus! Sanctus! Sanctus!"

Lux implevit spatium,
Multiformis colore;
Et audivit vocem suam
Resonare,

"Sanctus! Sanctus! Sanctus!"

Molliter angeli cantaverunt,

"Dominus Deus sabaoth,
Pleni sunt coeli et terra
Gloria tua!"

A SILVER THREAD

"Hosanna in excelsis!
Hosanna in excelsis!"
Vox in lumine transformat,
Et lumen canit,

"Sanctus! Sanctus! Sanctus!"

Lumen canit molliter,

"Dominus Deus sabaoth,
Pleni sunt coeli et terra
Gloria tua!"

Castissima virgo
Advenit in capellam;
Et angeli in vitro
Molliter cantaverunt.

SAINTE-CHAPELLE
2013 for Eric Whitacre

An innocent girl
Entered the chapel
And the angels in the glass
Softly sang,

"Hosanna in the highest!"

The innocent girl
Whispered,

"Holy! Holy! Holy!"

Light filled the chamber,
Many-colored light;
She heard her voice
Echo,

"Holy! Holy! Holy!"

Softly the angels sang,

"Lord God of Hosts,
Heaven and earth are full
Of your glory!"

A SILVER THREAD

"Hosannah in the highest!
Hosannah in the highest!"
Her voice became light,
And the light sang,

"Holy! Holy! Holy!"

The light sang softly,

"Lord God of Hosts,
Heaven and earth are full
Of your glory!"

An innocent girl
Entered the chapel
And the angels in the glass
Softly sang.

STARS IN HEAVEN
2013 for Toby Young

Stars in Heaven shining bright,
Dance across the black of night,
Sun and moon, and winds that blow,
Sing unto the earth below:
Parvula infinitas, mundum transformavit
    (Tiny infinity, you will transform the world)

Soil and stone, seed and flower,
Celebrate this holy hour;
Shepherds, kings, and mother mild,
Come adore the true Christ-Child!
Parvula infinitas, mundum transformavit
    (Tiny infinity, you will transform the world)

Child of Heaven, Son of Man,
Born before this world began;
Holy child so young, so old,
Save us as the prophets told.
Parvula infinitas, mundum transformavit
    (Tiny infinity, you will transform the world)

ST. GEORGE AND THE DRAGON,
An Oratorio
2013 for Timothy Powell

ASCALON
In old Silene, where ocean breezes blow
And cool the blazing desert sands below,
There was an ancient kingdom fair and grand;
But misery and fear had gripped that land
For cursed it was by dragon foul and fey
Until a hero came to save the day!
Or so the legends say…

But legends often only half-truths tell
And I alone know what indeed befell
That day when George, the Hero and the Saint,
Arrived to rescue Sabra from her fate.

This princess, by her father cruelly bound,
Was chained unto a pillar, to be found
And eaten by the dragon Ascalon,
Whom he believed had brought a curse upon
The kingdom of Silene.

I am that Ascalon, that dragon fell,
And now the turn is mine this tale to tell.
One morning when emerging from my lair
I heard a maiden crying in despair.
I am that Ascalon, that dragon free;
I heard her cry and listened silently.

SABRA
How could my father do this?
I begged him not to act
To kill his only daughter
Is a waste, and that's a fact!

He thinks the kingdom's cursed by dragons
Who demand a sacrifice!
I tried to tell him what was real,
That we need not pay this price!"

'You're just a child' he scolded,
'How could you understand?
The ancient prophecy is clear—
Now give the man your hands!'

How cruel is my destiny,
To be cut down in my youth!
An "ancient prophecy" indeed;
Even I can see the truth!

A SILVER THREAD

My father and his book are blind
I'm so angry I could spit!
I'm glad to leave a kingdom
That believes in such bull——Aaah!

ASCALON
Fear not, dear child, for I shall do no harm!
Here, let me loose the bonds upon your arm.
I overheard your cries – you are correct –
We dragons seek to heal and to protect.
The earth and all her creatures are our ward;
But men have turned, and put us to the sword.
We do not understand why this is so.
This fate is ours; but you are free to go.
Return ye home, and may you always see
That Ascalon shall at your service be!

SABRA
There is indeed a service, Lord,
That you may render me.
No longer trapped behind my walls
Am I content to be!

I want to fly!
Spread out your wings and carry me—and fly!
There's a whole world for me to see
So let's fly!

There's so much of the world to see
And wonders to explore;
I've read through each and every book
And still I must learn more!

But you could take me, Ascalon,
To places far away;
Your golden wings—they make you lord
Of all that you survey!

To ancient caves and mountaintops
And islands in the sea,
Your wings could take us anywhere!
Oh, will you carry me?

ASCALON
You are indeed a maiden wondrous rare
To seek a grand adventure *outremer!*
Around the world my wings shall carry thee
To satisfy your curiosity,
Oh, my princess Sabra!

She spun about and cried aloud for joy!
When of a sudden rushed on us a boy;
With sword unsheathed and armor shining bright
He thought himself the image of a knight.

A SILVER THREAD

GEORGE
Unhand that maiden,
Or I shall kill you, dragon, have no doubt!

ASCALON
But I could see a fear behind his eyes;
His armor, too, was ill-fit to his size.
The hands that gripped his sword were trembling,
And I could catch his voice a-mumbling:

GEORGE (aside)
The hero's gaze is always keen,
Prepared for dangers unforeseen.
His body healthy, fit and lean;
He keeps his sword and armor clean.

ASCALON
Young man, said I, why make this martial threat?
We two have not been introduced, and yet
You come into my home with sword out-drawn!
Sir Knight, I am the dragon Ascalon.
I am at your service!

GEORGE
You speak, Dragon
But I shall not listen,
For dragons lie.
It says so in this book.
I know what I must do.

The hero saves the damsel fair
From pirate's cave and dragon's lair.
He seeth past the villain's lies,
Instead believing his own eyes.

ASCALON
What sort of book has guided you this wise?
A hero must not always trust his eyes,
For eyes are but the windows of the mind;
Men see in shadows, yet to light are blind.
While some that seem so foul may yet prove fair,
And fair prove foul—a hero must beware!
Take dragonkind, *exemplo gratia:*
We have been healers for millennia.
I came to free this lake of pestilence,
And for it I am met with violence.
Thus has it lately been.

GEORGE
A healer, you say? Ha!
How can that be so?
You are a dragon,
And dragons are monsters!

ASCALON
How many other dragons have you met?
There be no beard upon your chin as yet—
Your hero's journey only just begun—
So pay ye heed to dragon Ascalon.

A SILVER THREAD

GEORGE
Enough!

> *A hero takes his sword in hand*
> *And rids the dragon from the land.*

Fair maiden, I shall save you!

ASCALON
He lunged upon me, brandishing his blade;
But his attack was easy to evade.
I spread my wings and yelled a mighty roar;
A plume of fire up to the heavens tore,
At which the boy recoiled in fear before
The dragon Ascalon!

GEORGE
You could have killed me, this I see.
Why, then, did you let me be?

ASCALON
The choice to deal out life or death is grave—
Consider whom to kill and whom to save.
> *A hero does not rush to kill.*
> *He waits to draw his sword until*
> *He sees his villain's spirit true,*
> *And only then knows what to do.*

GEORGE
But you attacked this maiden fair—
I thought her lucky I was there!

SABRA
You are mistaken, good Sir Knight,
For I can save myself!
This dragon is my teacher, sir;
I need no hero's help.

First my father made of me
A sacrifice of Hate;
Now you come to me assuming
You control my fate!

Well, I am not to be controlled—
No passive princess I!
Your silly storybooks are wrong
About both what and why.

I'm neither helpless nor a fool;
Your rules shall not this princess rule!

ASCALON
The world is bigger far than you can know;
A thousand thousand places can you go
And still not see the wonder of it all,
Until the very halls of Time shall fall.

A SILVER THREAD

Now, many legends speak of dragonkind;
But these are merely villains of the mind.
The dragon is a *symbol*, that is all,
Of inner ignorance, and shadowfall.

GEORGE
I see it now that I was wrong
To live on legend, myth, and song.
Forgive, if I've offended you;
I know now what I'm meant to do.
I only wish to do what's best
As I embark upon this quest
To be a hero just and true;
And I know how, because of you!

ASCALON
And so in time we two convinced the youth
'Twixt good and bad to go and seek the truth.
I'm proud to say a hero he became:
St. George the Dragonslayer is his name!

We saw the wondrous world, Sabra and I,
Until, at last, we had to say goodbye.
For many journeys I have been the guide,
But not for many more can I abide.

So, hero, use thy reason first;
By blindness shall you not be cursed.
Learn to pierce fair villain's guise,
And monsters' wisdom recognize.

I am that Ascalon, that dragon free
I keep the watch, and wait to mentor thee.
I am that Ascalon, that monster wise,
My vigil keeping 'till the last arise!

HAROMANNUM
2014 for Dan Forrest

H	A	R	O	M	A	N	N	U	M

H A R O M A N N U M		M
A		U
R		N
O	*En ándelo rha mánzanu*	N
M	*En dórmo nandrevénno*	A
A	*Shereh menán zheróvenu*	M
N	*An déstaran adéndo*	O
N		R
U		A
M U N N A M O R A H		H

HAROMANNUM
2014 for Dan Forrest

When you rest here in my enfolding,
When you sleep in the hollows of my heart,
My love, we two are merged as in one being,
And our spirits ascend together into Heaven.

A SILVER THREAD

NEW YEAR'S CAROL
2014 for Ola Gjeilo

After all the gifts have been opened,
After the candles all have burned down,
After the warmth comes the chill of the season;
After the carols, the winter wind's sound.

After all our friends have departed,
After the tinsel is all put away,
That is the time to reflect and remember—
The gifts of the season last more than one day.

The wheel of the year keeps turning, returning;
The sun, ever-dancing, shall lengthen the day.
Soon will the frostbite give way to the flower;
For under the snow waits the promise of May.

We hold in our hearts the joys of this season,
Warming our spirits as bitter winds blow;
Bringing to mind our soul, all that matters;
Of that which is hollow, in faith letting go.

SOLI DEO GLORIA!
2014 for Ola Gjeilo

For the spirit universal,
Force and matter elemental,
Word and worlds and stars coeval—
Soli Deo gloria!   To You alone the glory!

For the spirit of creation,
Nature, art, and inspiration,
Life, and light's illumination—
Soli Deo gloria!   To You alone the glory!

For the gift of human kindness,
Each to each a watchful witness,
Loving that dispels all darkness—
Soli Deo gloria!   To You alone the glory!

A SILVER THREAD

STELLA CLARA
2015 for Richard Waters

Stella clara,
Stella fulgens,
Primam stellam video:
Permittarne,
Possiemne,
Habere quod voveo?

Quod donatum
Ad beatum
Aëvum desidero?
Amor? Aurum?
Quies? Salus?
Immo, lassus, dormio.

Ecce! Donum
Fasque verum
Visum est dum somnio!
Stella clara,
Stella fulgens:
Dona me quod voveo!

STAR BRIGHT
STELLA CLARA
2015 for Richard Waters

Star light,
Star bright,
First star I see tonight:
I wish I may,
I wish I might,
Have the wish I wish tonight.

But what request
Would be the best
For happiness along life's quest?
True love? Or wealth?
Or peace? Or health?
Alas, all weary, I must rest.

Lo! While asleep,
A vision deep
Revealed to me the gift to keep!
Star light,
Shining bright:
Grant the wish I make tonight!

A SILVER THREAD

ETERNAL PROMISE
2015 for Doug Helvering

Ah, Love, more wondrous far than any force
That ever worked its pow'r upon a heart!
Ah, Love, you captor cruel, without remorse,
Why do you first ensnare, and then depart?
A glance becomes a touch; a touch, a kiss;
No food, nor sleep can calm the heartbeat's race!
In all the earth there be no greater bliss
Than thy belovéd's love, in love's embrace!
But love like this cannot endure through time.
Our interests fade, as fresh experience
Supplants our ex-obsession, once sublime,
And passion withers to expedience.
The only loves which last eternally
Are God's for us, and mine, belov'd, for thee.

#twitterlieder
2015 for James Eakin III

Act 1

1. BIRTHDAY
Today is my birthday!
A birth is such a wondrous event,
when the veil of eternity opens,
for just a moment,
and a new soul enters the world.

2. SCHOOLYARD
The schoolyard's happy, full of children
singing ring around the rosy,
and choosing teams for dodgeball.
School is fun, but summer's funner!

3. OMG
OMG! This totally creepy guy from biology class just
asked me to prom!
I totally said no-AS IF I would ever go out with HIM!
#eww #whyme :-(

4. SCHOLARS
Black-robed scholars sit, row upon row,
Waiting to hear their names called out,
As each is handed their future
With a smile and a handshake.

A SILVER THREAD

5. RISE OF SUN
At rise of sun the day unfolds;
Yet none here knows what bloom it holds.
Wends and ways
Of endless days
Concealed in blue and pink and gold.

Act 2

6. THE BIG NIGHT!
Tonight's the big night!
I've got the ring; I've made the reservations;
and starting tomorrow we two will be one
for the rest of our lives!!

7. SELFIE
Here we are
Standing in the doorway
Looking faabulous
Look at me
Look at us
Photo-bombing
Having a ball
Scrolling
Laughing
Tweeting
Deleting

8. BUSY
carpooltrafficgrabalattemorningmeetingconference
callworkthrulunchansweremailminorcrisisdoublelatte
carpooltrafficsuppertimechoirrehearsalwine

9. MERRY-GO-ROUND
Sit and talk with me a while.
Let's both step off the merry-go-round long enough
    to catch our breath
and remember why we love each other.

10. PEOPLE OF LIGHT
From our first day outside the womb
To final closure of the tomb
We strive for right
As people of light,
Enduring *ad infinitum.*

Act 3

11. BROTHERS OF THE HEART
We may not share the same blood, my friend,
    but we are brothers of the heart.
Best friends are family you choose for yourself.
I love you…

A SILVER THREAD

12. AUTO-CORRECT
Autumn leaves rustle
As another year cones to and end
Another tear oven to a send
Abridger year
Some other
Comes to amend
Duck auto-correct!

13. MOM
I went to visit mom today.
I needed to see her smile,
    hear the sound of her voice.
I had to tell her: now I understand
    to savor each moment!

14. FIBER
I don't understand anything, nothing at all.
But I'm beginning to know the value of family,
    of good friends, and of love...
oh, and fiber…

15. TREASURES
We storm and we stress and rushing past
Around us fly the moments fast.
Don't waste today
On yesterday,
But gather treasures that will last.

TWO PINES
2015 for John Muehleisen

Upon an ancient mountaintop there grow
A pair of pines—majestic, tall, and grand—
As cranes, at home where heaven touches earth.

A sea of mist enshrouds the vale below;
Unspoken dreams and secrets dark and deep
Beneath uncertain waters hidden lie.

But high above the mist the stars still shine
Their flick'ring light, until the sun shall rise
And splendid shatter all our darkening,

And two proud pines beneath the earth entwine;
Embracing roots, they gravel down to touch
The sacred fire—the source of life, of love.

A SILVER THREAD

WHAT IS THIS LIGHT?
2015 for Eric Barnum

What is this light that enlightens our darkness?
What is this joy that enjoins us to love?
How can infinity fit in such limits?
How can below welcome Heaven above?

How can the power that opened the heavens,
Founded the earth and scattered the stars,
How can the author of all of creation
Deign to abide where we, miserable, are?

What shall we do to prepare for his coming,
When all of our worship, our music, our arts
Fail, insufficient, to honor his glory?
All we need do is to open our hearts.

A WINTER'S SPELL
2015 for Tim Takach

On the old porch swing I set a spell,
For storing up cicadas' lulling buzz,
Hazy summer sunset lingering
All lazy, ripe, and heavy on the night.

Far too soon this light will turn to gold,
And fireflies will flee the waning day.
Copper leaves will choke the guttered eaves
As all the signs of summer fade from sight.

Soon the snows shall gather up the green,
A chill wind whistling through the branches
bare;
Silences in violet shadows fall,
Reflect, refract through gleaming prismic white.

How shall I endure this winter's chill,
When blizzard bites the blood and shivers all?
I'll remember then the spell I set
Upon the old porch swing in summer's light.

A SILVER THREAD

WHO AM I?
2015 for Jake Narverud

I
Who am I?
I am the voice of youth
Singing and dreaming,
Searching for the light.
Who am I?
I am the spirit of freedom
Stretching and learning,
Finding my truth.

With my friends beside me,
I can do anything!
With mentors to guide me
On my way,
I can discover
How I belong here;
I can discover
Who I really am.

II
Who am I?
I am a storm of feelings
Doubting, searching,
Making mistakes.
Who am I?
I am afraid, uncertain,
Stressed out, different,
On display.

Soon all my friends
Will say their goodbyes,
And all that I've known
Will fade away.
So many words
I've left unspoken…
Does anyone know
Who I really am?

This is the moment!
I'm tired of hiding.
These masks that I'm wearing
Are torn away.
I stand here before you
With my sisters and brothers,
Ready to show you
Who I really am!

III
Who am I?
I am the voice of the future
Singing and dreaming,
Shining my light!
Who am I?
I am the spirit of freedom,
Wings open wide
And ready to fly!

I'm ready to go;
There's no turning back now.
One chapter closes,
Another begins.
I'm ready to show
What I have to offer,
And the world will see
Who I really am!

A SILVER THREAD

I AM
2016 for Jake Narverud

I am the voice of youth.
Singing, dreaming,
Embracing the light.

I am the spirit of freedom.
Stretching, yearning,
Finding what's right.

I am a storm of feelings.
Doubting, searching,
Learning my way.

I am torn and troubled.
Different, uncertain,
Out on display.

I am the face of hope.
Singing, dreaming,
Shining my light.

So who is the one with their future in hand
And the power to make a change?
I am.

THE OTHER SIDE OF ETERNITY
2016 for Stuart Turnbull

Whenever there is birth or death,
The sacred veil between the worlds
Grows thin and opens slightly up
Just long enough for Love to slip,
Silent, either in or out
Of this our fragile, fleeting world,
Whence or whither a new home awaits.
And our beloved ones draw near,
In rapt anticipation, or
In weary gratitude, they stand;
Our loved ones stand so close, just here,
Right here, just on the other side
Of Eternity.

A SILVER THREAD

NORTHWOODS
2016 for Ola Gjeilo

Sapphire river born
  where clouds kiss mountain tops
Snow-capped towers rise
  ever upward
Auroral emerald ribbons blaze
  among countless stars
Gentle rains shower
  spires of conifer
The northwood wakes...

Blue-winged dragonflies hover
  over crystal lakes
Snow-melt trickling
  into summer
The northwood breathes

OVER THE RIDGE
2016 for Eric Barnum

Over the ridge
The summer sun sets
Colors tumbling
Sun strewn
An impossible tapestry
Of lavender
Vermillion
And golden satin
Glittering upon
A ribbon of water
As I take in
The long view down the river

This water flows
Through villages and towns
Past farm and mill
Through time
Into this valley pour
The joys and sorrows
The work and prayers
Of generations
This rugged land rises up
And tumbles down
A testament of ages
Majestic, wondrous, free

A SILVER THREAD

Over the ridge
The sun sets
And I reflect on my time
In this wholesome valley
My heart is full
My spirit free
As I take in once more
That long view down the river

SANCTUARY
2016 for Ola Gjeilo

Whenever I am weary,
When glass and steel and grey close in,
There is a place,
A valley, wide and green,
Amid the shadowed canyons,
Where my spirit roams free.

    The towers rise, the shadows fall,
    The traffic weaving through it all;
    Then I escape across the wall
    As if to answer a distant call…

Where paths lead, meandering,
Through field and wooded wild;
Where clear blue sky
Reflected in still water
Reminds me
Who I am.

A SILVER THREAD

SEASONS
2016 for Ola Gjeilo

Bright the sun in bluest shining;
Summer spreads in valleys greenly.
Lovers sing their new-found pining;
Time itself slows down to greet me.

Autumn air comes crisp and blowing
Leaves from green to golden turning;
Hearts all full, and eyes all glowing
Gather round the hearth-fire burning.

Night grows longer, darkness deeper,
Cold winds howl when comes the Winter;
White of snow by moonlight tempered,
Bearing hope for Spring to enter.

Flowers bloom with showers falling,
All the world reveals its yearning;
Nature sings—I hear her calling:
Round and round the seasons turning.

THEN, AND STILL
2016 for Susan LaBarr

We were married in late September,
Among the changing leaves;
Crimson banners in the courtyard
Heralded our union.
We were so happy then.

The music we shared brought us together,
A duet most unlikely.
Work and home and son and daughter,
Busy in joy and love.
How normal we seemed, then.

But who could know what fate awaited
Our little family of four?
A spectre came and dwelt among us,
And robbed us of our joy.
And then, we were only three.

But time has passed, and wounds have healed,
Leaving scars behind;
But scars, like talismans, remind us
What was, and what yet may be,
That we loved, and love you still.

A SILVER THREAD

WINTERTIDE
2016 for Ola Gjeilo

Stillness comes when snow is falling,
Cov'ring all in solemn white;
Lines of grey from hearth-fires rising,
Gath'ring all in restful night.

Spirit dwells in deep reflection,
Autumn cares to lay aside,
Finding signs of new direction
In the still of Wintertide.

While outside the cold wind blowing,
Swirling, restless raw and rime,
Here inside a wave is growing,
Biding, silent, all in time.

After Winter's meditation
Gates of nature burst apart;
Comes the Springtime's inspiration,
Flowing from the ready heart.

POOR IN SPIRIT
from *Tuvayhun: Beatitudes for a*
  Wounded World
2017 for Kim Andre Arnesen

Blessed are the poor in spirit: for theirs is the kingdom of
Heaven. (Matthew 5:3)

I am poor, yes;
I am poor in spirit.

In despair I weep for the world I see,
A world of poverty, of misery,
Of loneliness profound;
A world of hate, of sad division,
And of shocking cruelty,
Where trolls well-fed and liars bold
Erode our sense of shared humanity,
Setting sister against brother,
Neighbor against neighbor,
Race against race,
Faith against faith,
Nation against nation.

A SILVER THREAD

How long must we wait, O Lord? How long?
When will Your promised Kingdom come?
How can one NOT be poor in spirit
When lies become truth,
And Truth lies, rejected?
When saints are silenced
And villains grow mighty?
While mumbling leaders dither and look away?

Why must we wait for the coming of the Kingdom,
My sisters and my brothers?
Why must we wait, O Lord?
For when one is poor in Spirit,
One is poor indeed.

LEAVING YOU BEHIND
**from *Tuvayhun: Beatitudes for a
    Wounded World***
2017 for Kim Andre Arnesen

*Blessed are those who mourn: for they will be comforted.
(Matthew 5:4)*

Leaving you behind
Is the hardest thing I've ever done.
Leaving you behind,
You who were my everything.

Keep the memory of me,
And may my memory be a blessing—
The songs, the smiles, the laughter—
Every little thing that made you love me.

Love is powerful
In life as well as death;
For even as I die,
Eternal becomes my love for you.

Leaving you behind
Only makes our bonding stronger,
Vaster, longer,
Every day, in every way.

A SILVER THREAD

BLESSED ARE THE MEEK
from *Tuvayhun: Beatitudes for a Wounded World*
2017 for Kim Andre Arnesen

Blessed are the meek: for they will inherit the earth.
(Matthew 5:5)

Mama, I don't want to sleep!
So many things I want to do,
So many things I want to see,
I couldn't ever go to sleep!
Mama, will you sing to me?

> Go to sleep, my precious child,
> And lay aside your worries.
> Tomorrow is another day
> To grow and learn, and love and play.
> Tomorrow, all the world shall be
> Just as it was today, you'll see.

Mama, I don't want to sleep!
I want to jump! I want to dance!
I want to sing the whole night through!
I couldn't think of sleep at all.
Mama, May I sing with you?

Go to sleep, my restless one,
And still your stirring spirit
The silent stars shall dance tonight
And greet the sun in morning light.
Tomorrow all the world shall leap;
But only if you go to sleep!

(I pray to God who dwells above
To watch you closely as you sleep,
And grant you all the joys you seek.
The world is darker than you know,
But blessed, blessed are the meek!)

Tomorrow morning, when you wake,
The world will be made new again;
But you will be a little taller,
And the big, wide world just a little smaller.
Tomorrow the world is yours to keep;
But tonight, my darling, precious child,
Tonight, my sweet one, go to sleep!

A SILVER THREAD

SING OUT YOUR TRUTH
from *Tuvayhun: Beatitudes for a Wounded World*
2017 for Kim Andre Arnesen

Blessed are those who hunger and thirst for righteousness: for they will be filled. (Matthew 5:6)

In all that we are,
It is better by far
To follow our star,
And sing out our truth.

When things can't get worse,
We hunger and thirst
For the last to be first;
And so we sing out our truth.

We sing for the poor.
We sing for the weak.
We sing for the helpless,
The hopeless, the meek.
We sing out the truth
Against hunger and hate.
We sing out for justice
Before it's too late!

And in all that we do
For these, and for you,
The whole dark night through
We're gonna sing out our truth!

A SILVER THREAD

FORTY DAYS AND FORTY NIGHTS
from *Tuvayhun: Beatitudes for a
    Wounded World*
2017 for Kim Andre Arnesen

*Blessed are the merciful: for they will be shown mercy.
(Matthew 5:7)*

Forty days and forty nights
The bombs rained down.
School, road, marketplace,
The world we knew
Now only dust and blood.

    Who will tend the orchard, with harvest coming on?
    Who will greet the sunrise on the hill?
    Will we ever taste again the spices of our home?
    Who can know it if we ever will?

Forty days and forty nights
We fled, frightened;
Desert, mountain, stormy sea…
Silent strangers
Passing by your door.

Will we be forgotten as we journey far from home?
Will we find a safer place to stay?
Will new neighbors welcome us
   as brothers and as friends?
Or will they scoff and send us on our way?

Forty days and forty nights
We've settled now,
Broken, worn out, waiting.
All was lost,
Except our hope.

May we sit and share with you the story of our journey,
And of our hope, and hardships overcome?
May we help you tend your orchard,
   when harvest's coming on?
May we share with you the spices of our home?

A SILVER THREAD

THE FACE OF GOD
**from *Tuvayhun: Beatitudes for a
Wounded World***
2017 for Kim Andre Arnesen

*Blessed are the pure in heart: for they will see God.
(Matthew 5:8)*

Blessed are the pure in heart,
For they shall see God.

But I wonder...
Will the God I see
Look at all like me?

For we have many names, many faces,
Different mothers, different races.
How can we, who are so many,
Have a God resembling any of us?
I wonder...

And when I smile at the face of God,
Will God be smiling back at me?
Am I worthy of that smile? Are we?
We need not wonder...

For God has many hands—our hands.
And God has many hearts—our hearts.
And when we look upon each other's faces
We see the face of God.

PEACE IS FIRE!
from *Tuvayhun: Beatitudes for a Wounded World*
2017 for Kim Andre Arnesen

Blessed are the peacemakers: for they will be called children of God. (Matthew 5:9)

Peace is not a silent state
That comes upon us from within—
Serene, detached, oblivious.

Peace is not a force like rain
That comes, unbidden, from above—
Gentle, enfolding, natural.

Peace is fire! Peace is passion!
Peace requires strength of will,
A certain courage, a heart of iron,
A force abiding to fulfill.

Peace is not a foregone fate;
For peace, like war, must be waged—
Mindfully, deliberately,
With arms ever ready,
And eyes wide open.

The waging of peace is our highest call.

A SILVER THREAD

HOLD MY HAND
from *Tuvayhun: Beatitudes for a Wounded World*
2017 for Kim Andre Arnesen

Blessed are those who are persecuted for righteousness sake: for theirs is the kingdom of heaven. (Matthew 5:10)

Brothers and sisters, gather round,
And hear the words I say,
For the world can be a better place
If we hold hands today.

Hold my hand and stand with me,
And face the tide together;
And we will change the world today,
Tomorrow, and forever.

Hold my hand against injustice;
Hold my hand and stand with me.
Hold my hand against division;
Just take my hand and see.

Hold my hand to conquer hatred;
Hold my hand and stand with me.
The troubles of the world will melt,
And we will blessed be.

Brothers and sisters, gather round,
And hear the words we say,
For the world can be a better place
If we hold hands today.

A SILVER THREAD

MUSE
2017 for Daniel Elder

In silence,
Sitting, staring,
Awaiting a cue,
Hearing the music,
Fully-formed in ringing ears;
But leaden fingers falter...

Finished pages tossed aside,
While empty lines stare back still,
Like barbed-wire fences
Trapping the silence,
Barring the music beyond.

And she wonders...
Will her Muse
Will this, her music, speak the poet's heart?
Will others rise to sing along?
And who will hear her song?

And then the music flows again,
Busy hands make Light!
In love she spins the pitches
Into threads of phrase,
Of lift and line,
And into cords of melody.

Notes like beads of pearl and jet
Shimmer in the warp and weft
Of staff and stem,
As slowly she weaves
The tapestry of her masterpiece.

The once-empty lines
Now become a scaffold,
Linking past to present,
Building ever-upward,
As she adds her voice
To the chorus of the ages.

In silence,
For just a moment,
With finished pages all around,
Sitting, sighing,
She wonders...
For truly wondrous it is
To weave together all the hearts
Of those who write,
Of those who sing,
And of those who hear the song!

A SILVER THREAD

THE PEACEMAKER
2017

Take her up, Cowboy, from where she lies,
And feel her power and her weight;
Cradle her gently in the curve of your left hand
As your right hand opens her gate...

Slowly and tenderly, using your thumb,
Draw back the hammer to half-cock;
Spin her 'round, Cowboy, and hear her click,
As her cylinder starts to unlock...

> You've got a Peacemaker, Colt .45,
> Treat her well, Cowboy, and she'll keep you alive.
> Her smooth single-action is simply the best–
> She's the revolver that tamed the Wild West!

Gently now, Cowboy, in the palm of your hand,
Lay her on her left side;
Expose her open chamber
And slip your cartridge inside...

Six chambers she has, ready to fire;
But only five give the old girl,
For it's how he uses that empty chamber
That a Cowboy can change the world.

You've got a Peacemaker, Colt .45,
Treat her well, Cowboy, and she'll keep you alive.
Her smooth single-action is simply the best–
She's the revolver that tamed the Wild West!

PEREGRINUS, PEREGRINOR
2017 for Susan LaBarr

Peregrinus, peregrinor,
Semper via ubique;
Mirabilia video,
Audio et aufero.

Arcana, et graviora,
Sequor sapientiam:
Non intersum sed intersumus,
Maior me est saeculum.

Muri facile struuntur,
Sed includunt nos ipsos.
Cantemus canticum nostrum
Dum possumus libere.

A WANDERER, I WANDER
PEREGRINUS, PEREGRINOR
2017 for Susan LaBarr

A wanderer, I wander,
Always and everywhere;
Wonders I behold,
I listen and I learn.

Secrets, and deeper things,
And wisdom have I found:
I matter not; it is We who matter,
The age is greater than I.

Walls are easily built,
But imprison us alone.
Let us sing our song
Boldly while we are able.

A SILVER THREAD

SO BRIGHT THE STAR
2017 for Ola Gjeilo

Timeless Child,
Born of my body,
Reconciling God to man,
So bright the Star
That shines tonight in the Heavens!

Gloria in excelsis Deo!
Glad tidings the Angels proclaim!
So bright the Star!

What is this news the Angels bring?
Who is this Child who is Savior and King?
Let us run to greet the Savior!
So great our joy!
So bright the Star!

STORGE, PHILIA, EROS, AGAPE
2017

στοργή

Sitting all together,
Table spread with joy;
One hand takes another,
Reaching across the generations
Gathering, singing, sharing.

φίλια

Partner in adventure,
Harbor in a stormy sea,
In all we do, my good friend.
Laughter is our language.
I love you like a brother; like a sister;
And you love me.

ἔρως

Embracing you,
Revealing my deepest, secret self to you,
Opening to you alone
Safe in your enfolding arms.

A SILVER THREAD

ἀγάπη

Always love, forever love,
Given freely, offered up;
Across all space and time
Perfect and
Eternal.

LOVE

TONIGHT I DANCE ALONE
2017 for Mårten Janssen

On an early summer evening
A man and a boy
Stood before a mirror
Looking in...
"Brother," said the boy,
"How do you tie a tie like that?"
"Left over right and up on through.
You'll get it right, when you wear a tie
On your wedding day!"

Tonight we dance in the moonlight,
My bride and I.
Tonight the moon is made for us,
To shine on us alone.
Tonight we'll kiss by the firelight
In the forest we love.

On an early summer evening
The man and a girl
Stood at the front door,
Looking out...
"Daddy," said the girl,
"Why are you all dressed up like that?"
"Your mother and I are going out
To fancy dinner, then off to dance
For our anniversary."

A SILVER THREAD

Tonight we dance in the starlight,
Your mother and I.
Tonight we toast two dozen years
Of life, of love, of joy.
Tonight we'll kiss in the candlelight,
In gratitude.

On an early summer evening
An old man and a boy
Walked to the edge of the driveway,
Step by step...
"Grandpa," said the boy,
"Why you wearin' that red bow tie?"
"It was your grandmother's favorite.
I wore it on our wedding day."
"Grandpa," said the boy,
"Will you see her, in the forest?"
"You never know.
Those woods are magic!"

Soon we will dance in the God-light,
My love and I.
Soon will the moon be ours again,
And the endless shining stars
In the halls of heaven.
Soon, my love, very soon;
But tonight, one last time,
Tonight I dance alone.

WAS IT WORTH IT? (An Irish song)
2017

They promised milk and honey,
They promised we'd be free,
And they promised boon and bounty;
But there's only misery.

For all her fertile farmland,
For all her rivers blue,
This country's hope and promise
Are but for a lucky few.

We came here in our thousands
Escaping want and woe;
But I wonder, was it worth it,
That we ever chose to go?

I have searched for work and wages,
For to earn my daily bread;
But "No Irish Need Apply here!"
All the factory door-signs said.

The story's all the same here,
No matter where we roam;
From Baltimore to Boston
It's so hard to make a home.

A SILVER THREAD

We crossed the sea all hopeful
To escape our want and woe;
But I wonder, was it worth it,
That we ever chose to go?

For in spite of all her hardship,
And the British iron hand,
My true home is where my heart is,
In dear old Ireland;

Where the home-fires still are burning,
And the green grows all around;
In the sacred hills of Erin,
Therein my heart is bound.

But America's my home now
And I'm on my way out West
To the gold of California,
Right along with all the rest.

Oh I left my ma in Galway
Left my wife in Baltimore,
And I'm off to seek my fortune;
Heaven knows what lies in store.

Men are leaving in their thousands
To find their fortunes fair;
And I wonder, is it worth it,
That now I journey there?

BLESSED ARE
2018 for James Eakin III

Blessed are the peacemakers,
  for they shall be called the children of God.

Blessed are they who speak out against injustice,
  for they are makers of peace.

Blessed are they who stand up for the forgotten,
      the oppressed,
  for they are makers of peace.

Blessed are they who offer up their lives in service
      of the other,
  for they are makers of peace.

Blessed are they who welcome the stranger,
      in memory of their own wanderings,
  for they are makers of peace.

Blessed are they who toil for the greater good,
  for they are makers of peace.

Blessed also are they who offer up even
      the simple dignity of a smile,
  for they too are makers of peace.

A SILVER THREAD

Blessed are they who care for the earth
    and all her creatures,
  for they are servants of peace.

Blessed are they that teach,
  for truly they are the teachers of peace.

Blessed are they with courage to speak their truth,
  for they are the guardians of peace.

Blessed are they who comfort the afflicted,
    and attend the dying,
  for they are bearers of peace.

Blessed are they who explore the inner silences,
  for they are icons of deep, abiding peace.

Rejoice, O Peacemakers, and be exceedingly glad,
  for as great as is your service here on earth,
    greater still shall be your reward in heaven! Amen.

CALLED TO REJOICE!
2018 for David Dickau

So many people, so many words,
So many heart-dreams dying, unheard,
Lost in the din of the push and the pull;
Empty we wander past, blind to the full
Infinite wonders, the great and the small—
How is a person to compass it all?

Ah, but with Music my heart can soar free,
To echo and magnify all that I see.
With Music, divisions can all fall away,
And blindnesses vanish in light of the day.

Music is language transcending all lands;
Music unites us—all voices, all hands.
Music is spirit, the voice of all arts,
Swelling and growing in myriad hearts.
Music has power to silence all strife;
Music is healing and loving and life.

Inspired by Music our hearts can soar free
Across the green valley, 'cross mountain and sea;
With Music we celebrate our humanity,
Standing together, voice upon voice,
Gathered in harmony, called to rejoice!

A SILVER THREAD

COLT .45
2018

The West was a wild and a dangerous place.
The way things were going it was such a disgrace.
Dark-hearted scoundrels and nature untamed
Were the law of the land; until the Peacemaker came.

    So I got me a Peacemaker, Colt .45.
    You treat your gun well and she'll keep you alive.
    Her smooth single-action is patented best—
    She's the revolver that tamed the Wild West!

Now I shot all my enemies, and some of my friends;
The game is all gone; the wars' at an end;
The Injuns are settled; the rustlers' deceased…
So how come I still don't feel any peace?

    So I got me a Peacemaker, Colt .45.
    You treat your gun well and she'll keep you alive.
    Her smooth single-action is patented best—
    She's the revolver that tamed the Wild West!

Often I wonder as I wander, alone,
Past one more ghost-town, another grave-stone:
That having the Peacemaker came with a cost;
We tamed the Wild West, but the best—it was lost.

So I got me a Peacemaker, Colt .45.
You treat your gun well and she'll keep you alive.
Her smooth single-action is patented best—
She's the revolver that tamed the Wild West!

Now all that's left is myself and my gun,
Alone as I ride to the setting sun;
Nothing remains but my own peace to make.
There's just one more life for this pistol to take.

I got me a Peacemaker, Colt .45.
I treated her well, and she kept me alive.
But now that she's come to the end of her quest,
She's the revolver that puts me to rest.

A SILVER THREAD

THE HALLSTATT SUMMER CAROL
2018

Halsbands-Herr und
Herr des Fibels,
Schildes-Herr und
Herr des Schwertes,
Seid willkommen,
Kommt mit uns!

Salve, Rex Solstitii,
Domine Aestatis!
Agricolae et bellatores
Hodie otiantur!

Hirschen-Herr und
Herr des Ebers,
Salzes-Herr und
Herr des Eisens,
Seid willkommen,
Jagdt mit uns!

Salve, vafer Venator,
Domine Cornuum!
Tibi supplicationes
Agimus pro mensa!

Berges-Herr und
Herr der Höhle,
Helden-Herr und
Herr der Völker,
Seid willkommen,
Tanzt mit uns!

   Veni, salta nobiscum,
   Domine Amoris!
   Trade te, conjunge nobis
   Festive in choro!

   Flamma sacra ardescit
   In medio anulo;
   Veni, Princeps, et incende
   Ignes in occulto!

Metes-Herr und
Herr des Blutes,
Feuers-Herr und
Herr des Herzens,
Seid willkommen,
Bleibt bei uns!

A SILVER THREAD

THE HALLSTATT
SUMMER CAROL
2018

Lord of Torque and
Lord of Fibula,
Shield-Lord, and
Lord of Sword,
Be welcome here,
Come with us!

   Welcome King of the Solstice,
   Summer-Lord!
   Both farmers and warriors
   Take their ease today!

Stag-Lord and
Lord of the Boar,
Salt-Lord and
Lord of Iron,
Be welcome here,
Hunt with us!

   Welcome, wily Hunter,
   Hornéd Lord!
   We give thanks to you
   For the bounty of our table!

Dread Lord of
Mine and Mountain,
Lord of Hero, and
Common Folk the same,
Be welcome here,
Dance with us!

Come, dance with us,
Lord of Love!
Surrender, and join us
In our merry circle!

The sacred flame grows brighter
In the center of our ring;
Come, O Prince, and ignite
The secret fires within!

Lord of Mead and Lord of Blood,
Fire-Lord, and
Lord of all Hearts,
Be welcome here,
Stay with us!

A SILVER THREAD

HOSHANA!
2018 for Connor Koppin

> *Hoshana*!
> In our misery we cry—
> *Hoshana*!
> Here, at the end of hope, we cry!
> *Hoshana*!

Another sunrise over the hills of home;
For us, another day of danger.
No food, nor light, nor hope for tomorrow;
Everywhere is desolation.
> *Hoshana*! Keep us safe!
Our children look up with fearful eyes;
We know what we must do.
> *Hoshana*! Keep us safe!

Another sunrise over unfamiliar hills;
For us, a painful journey.
Northward, ever northward in the night,
To cross the river into freedom.
> *Hoshana*! Guide our way!
Our children walk with hopeful steps;
How much farther must we go?
> *Hoshana*! Guide our way!

We've come so far, we've made our way;
From blood and hunger fled away.
Across the hills and burning sands;
Today we cross the borderlands
To a land of plenty we could share…
But we… we are not welcome there?
Oh, *Hoshana*!

Another sunrise over prison walls;
Captives in the land of freedom.
Our children, torn from us in terror,
Cry out, alone, and we are helpless.
  Hoshana! Keep them safe!
How much more must we endure?
We cannot stay here; nor can we return.
  Hoshana! In misery we cry!
May we not share with you the story of our journey?
May we not find a new home here with you?
  Hoshana! Guide their way!

KOLIBRI
2018

Rare and wonderful,
Small wings a blur,
Fast as a whisper she appears,
Full of mystery,
Hovering there
For only a moment—
Time stands still.

Her audience is fleeting.
She brings a welcome blessing,
A healing for the heart,
A reminder to the spirit
That the world is good,
That love is real,
And all will be whole again.

How can such a creature
So small, so fragile,
Fill such an emptiness?
I wonder, and once again
Set out my broken heart,
Waiting for her return, saying,
"Come! Here is sweet food!"

LIFT OUR LAMPS
2018

When the world is weak and weary
    And the flames of war are fanned,
In the midst of devastation
    Wrought by hate and evil hand,
We have fought and died for freedom
    In the blood and sweat and sand.
On a hundred shores we've fallen
    And still in Peace we stand.
America, America
    Meets History's demand;
On a hundred shores we've fallen
    And still in Peace we stand.

'Tis the hope of all our peoples
    In every broken place
That among our many blessings
    Are forgiveness, peace, and grace;
That war will never more approach
    Our homelands to deface;
That our enemies be neighbors,
    And our walls fall to embrace.
America, America,
    May we see no creed or race;
May our enemies be neighbors,
    And our walls fall to embrace.

A SILVER THREAD

While still indeed we wrestle
    As we try to do what's right,
And although our hearts be heavy,
    Our destiny is bright.
We must stand in hope united
    And for peace and justice fight,
As we lift our lamps into the darkness
    Bringing forth the light.
America, America
    Is a beacon in the night,
As we lift our lamps into the darkness
    Bringing forth the light!

OUR NAME IS PRIDE
2018

We've hidden ourselves, endured the shame;
We've lived false lives, the truth unnamed.
We've lost our partners, lovers, friends;
But this is not where our story ends.
Their courage has testified, showing us all—
We stand on their shoulders, and issue our call:

> Our name is Pride
> We are Diversity
> Our name is Strength
> We are Unity
> No one gets to say who we are
> No one gets to make us hide
> We decide what power we have
> Our name is Pride

Our brothers and sisters have struggled long
To lift up their voices, just to belong.
So many came forward and into the light,
Guiding our way toward justice and right.
Their courage has testified, calling us all
To stand on their shoulders,
Stand strong and stand tall!

A SILVER THREAD

Our name is Pride
We are Diversity
Our name is Strength
We are Unity
No one gets to say who we are
No longer can they stem the tide
We decide what power we have
Our name is Pride

PSALM 42
2018 for Jonathan Young

Like a deer who longs for running water,
  My soul it searches for you, O God!
My soul is athirst for the living God;
  Oh where and when shall he appear?

My tears are my food both day and night;
  I pour out my soul when I think of You.
Why so full of burdens, my soul?
  Why are you troubled so deep within?

Put your trust in the living God
  Whose springs of water are deep beyond deep.
Give thanks to Him who is your help,
  Who was, who is, and yet shall be.

All day long they say to me,
  "Where is now your living god?"
My foes they strike and break my bones
  And laughing mock me to my face.

Yet I recall in former days
  These same tormentors singing praise,
When once I led the multitude
  Into the holy house of God.

A SILVER THREAD

My soul indeed is heavy, Lord;
  And burdens rise to break me down;
And I have cause to wonder, Lord,
  Am I forgotten here, alone?

But the song of God still sings in me;
  My prayers by day and night arise;
And like the deer my soul will drink
  Of the living waters of the Lord.

Put your trust in the living God,
  For I will yet give thanks to Him
Who is the help of my countenance,
  My savior, and my God!

ROW, RED'S MEN, ROW!
2018 for Connor Koppin

REFRAIN:

Skeggöld, skálmöld,   skildir'ru klofnir—
Vindöld, vargöld,   áðr veröld steypisk!

An axe age, a sword age,   shields will be shattered—
A wind age, a wolf age,   ere the world ends!

VERSES:

Row, Red's men, row,   Row the whale-road wide!
Our sights are set for Vinland;   Ever West we ride!

Banished, never broken,   From the fjords we flew;
Our journey long and labored,   Our spirits stout and true.

Warriors we wander;   We ride the wending wind.
Thrice Thor did thunder   When left we Thorvald's kin.

Set the paling sail,   To seize the salty spray.
Ever West we journey;   Bold Erik knows the way!

Our ship is strong and sturdy   From dragon-stem to stern;
Our hearts are red and ready;   For battle-blood we burn!

A SILVER THREAD

Behind is raging Ægir;   Rán she roils ahead.
Swords and spirits sharpened,   Ready for the red!

The greening vales of Vinland   Call across the sea;
To each she offers bounty,   From thralldom to be free.

If we should fail to find her   And slip beneath the sea,
May Ođinn weigh us worthy   Valhallar all to be!

STAND UP!
2018 for Gerald Gurss

When the world gets you down
And there's trouble going 'round,
When you're thrown down to the ground,
You've got to stand up.

When it seems every day
That we've gone and lost our way,
Then you know I'm going to say
You've got to stand up.

> CHORUS
> Stand up and speak your truth;
> Stand up or step aside.
> Stand up and speak your truth;
> Speak up with pride!
>
> Stand up and speak your truth,
> Coming out or stepping in;
> Stand up and speak your truth;
> Let it begin!

When someone you know
Has cut you down real low;
If you want your light to show
You've got to stand up.

A SILVER THREAD

On the street or in the square,
In the courthouse, on the stair,
There's injustice everywhere,
So you've got to stand up.

CHORUS

When you're feeling mighty small…
When it seems you're going to fall…
When old evil's standing tall…
When hope can only crawl…
When they're building that damned wall…
When you want to help them all…
You've got to stand up and answer that call!

CHORUS

STARS WITHOUT NUMBER
2018 for Julian Bryson

We flicker…
We burn…
We shimmer…
Shine!

Stars beyond all number
Dance in countless Heavens;
Soaring and spinning in slow anticipation,
Dancing as we burn and wait…

Which burning brother, which spinning sister,
Chosen by the Dancing Master,
Will brighter burn than any star
Has ever shone in any age
Or span of universe?

Oh, I could be that Light,
For shepherds as for kings this night,
Guiding to that humble space
Where Shadow must give way to Grace;
Where Father gives the gift of Son,
Creation and Creator one!

We watch…
We wait…
We wish…
We shine!

A SILVER THREAD

TAKE THE TRAIN
2018 for Ivo Antognini

Sitting in the crowded station,
Minutes turning into hours;
Unsure of my destination,
Hours into days devour.
Many trains are all-aboarding,
Each to different destiny.
Whither is my soul towarding?
West or East? Which one for me?

> Take the train!
> Seize the moment!
> Make the journey!
> Life awaits!
> Don't hesitate!
> Embrace the yearning!
> Now's the moment!
> Take the train!

Destiny is full of choices:
Voyages both great and small,
Many pathways, many voices.
One must only heed the call.
You're the sum of all your journeys,
Each one teaching wisdom new.
Leave the station! Time is turning!
Take the train, and live anew!

Take the train!
Seize the moment!
Make the journey!
Life awaits!
Don't hesitate!
Embrace the yearning!
Now's the moment!
Take the train!

A SILVER THREAD

THE WAY OF TRUST
2018 for Andrea Ramsey

All around us
In this broken, fragile world,
Are broken, fragile people
Fumbling on their way,
Falling, unthinking,
Into old and well-worn pathways
That cleave the world, dividing
The familiar and the fey.

But the sword that divides
Cuts self as well as others;
Sisters and brothers
Cling to yesterday.
We must see
The world with eyes unclouded,
Look toward tomorrow
And seek the middle way.

The way of trust,
The way of hope unbounded,
The way of true affection
Must be our path today;
The way is hard,
Commands a higher calling
To rise above our nature
And embrace the middle way!

TILL DEATH US DO PART
2018 for Kim Andre Arnesen

"In the presence of God I choose you
To have and to hold
From this day forward,
For better, or for worse,
For richer, for poorer,
In sickness and in health,
To love and cherish,
So long as we both shall live.
All this do we vow and promise…"
As we begin our journey
On this our happiest day.

The vows we speak today in joy
By time and trials are tested:
But love abides
In good times and in bad,
Until that saddest day
When one of us
Must close the other's eyes
And say goodbye.

A SILVER THREAD

Too soon, my love, too soon,
Your sickness and your health
Took the better from the worst
Till death parted us.
Too soon, my love, too soon.
I loved loving you;
I cherish having cherished you.
My honor ever was and is to honor you,
Until we meet again.

UNDER THE SUGAR MOON
2018

Under the Sugar Moon,
My love and I,
We lie with limbs entwined;
We give our flowers each to each
Under the Flower Moon.

Under the Strawberry Moon,
My love and I,
We ply the earth and toil;
We plant our garden and wait,
Under the Thunder Moon.

Under the Barley Moon,
My love and I,
We sigh and gather in;
We give our thanks and share our plenty
Under the Harvest Moon.

Under the Cold and Snowy Moon,
My love and I,
We lie with limbs entwined.
Under the Storm Moon, the Hunger Moon,
We lie entwined, and wait to find
The dawning of the long-awaited spring
Under the Sugar Moon.

A SILVER THREAD

WHEN WE LOVE
2018 for Elaine Hagenberg

The towering tree spreads his greening canopy
—A veil between the soil and sky—
Not in selfish vanity,
But the gentle thrush to shade and shelter.
So it is with love.

For when we love,
Simply love,
Even as we are loved,
Our weary world can be transformed.

The busy thrush builds her nest below
—A fortnight's work to weave and set—
Not for herself alone,
But her tender brood to shield and cherish.
And so it is with love.

For when we love,
Simply love,
Even as we are loved,
Our weary world can be transformed
Into the Kingdom of God!

If we but love,
Simply love,
Even as we ourselves are loved,
Our weary world will be transformed
Into the Kingdom of God!

A SILVER THREAD

REQUIEM RESPONSES
2018 for Mårten Jansson

I. INTROITUS
Or so the living pray
For their beloved dead,
And pure is their intention so to do;

But the living only see
As through a glass, darkly,
the great Enigma that awaits beyond,

Where glimpse of Truth, and grief,
And darker shadows still,
Entwine to weave the old familiar words.

Do not grieve, my friends,
That I have gone away,
For I have crossed into Infinity

Where now I know the answers
To questions hidden then
When still I stood where now you stand and
grieve.

II. KYRIE

Cry not in anguished voices
For gifts already given;
He sees the pain our choices
Inflict on hopes of heaven.

It is we who must have mercy,
Each one upon another;
Whyever would one curse
Him who is himself our brother?

The Lord has mercy boundless
And that He freely gives;
Our fear of death is groundless,
For he who died now lives!

III. DIES IRAE

On that day of weeping
There is no weeping here;
For here there is only Heaven,
Here there is only joy,
And God is only Love.

The torments we fear are real;
For once we are enfolded
In the perfect love of God
—Gentle, boundless, freely given—
We remember past transgressions,

A SILVER THREAD

Our selfishness and self-delusion.
To stand in our shame
Before such terrible love
Is exquisite torment,
And we become our own tormentors.

But just as stone is worn away
By endless washing of the sea,
So the stubborn spines of our illusion
And the armor of our pride
Are sanded down to the raw
—However long it may require—
Until, at last,
We lay aside our heavy burdens
And accept the indescribable gift.

Abandon your illusions
And die before you die,
So on that day you cross the veil
And slip into eternity,
You will fall headlong
Into Love, into Joy,
Into the waiting arms of God.

IV. SANCTUS
I stand upon a landscape of infinity,
Vast, yet intimate.
In the distance I see the Presence,
Glowing with impossible light;
The thrum of hosts beyond number
Surrounds me as they sing
Their endless Holy! Holy!

Wave upon wave of Love
Emanate from that light;
While lightning flashes
Of golden evangelion
Carry prayers and blessings
To and from the Presence.
Holy! Holy!

Drawn into the Light,
I fade,
I lose myself...
Holy! Holy!
There is no I
There is only We
Only the endless and eternal One

I cannot describe...
Words fail...
Holy! Holy! Holy!

A SILVER THREAD

V. LUX AETERNA
Light is always and everywhere!

Light,
Bursting forth from the hearts
 of a billion billion stars;
Reflecting and refracting
 across infinite space;

Light,
In the prismic flashing fire
 from a diamond's heart;
In the crackling bolt
 of white-hot lightning;
In the soft golden glow
 of summer sun,
Softened to silver
 by the smiling moon;

Light,
Carried in the mouths
 of countless angels
Sent from the source
 of all Love;
Pouring from the face of God
 a blessing for all time;

And Light,
Shining forth
 from our own fragile hearts,
Magnifying multitudes,
 liberating infinite Love.

VI. PIE JESU
Eternal Rest.
Eternal Rest?
No rest for me;
My journey has only just begun!

VII. IN PARADISUM
Here, on the other side of eternity,
I need not await your coming,
For we are already together,
As always we have been.

Here, on the other side of eternity,
Time and space have no meaning,
For past and future fall away,
And there is only ever now.

Here, on the other side of eternity,
There are no limits of thought,
Or dimension, or understanding,
For here, all is known,
All is compassed,
And all is infinite, perfect Love.

A SILVER THREAD

THE WATCHES OF THE NIGHT
2018

Of late I awaken in the watches of the night,
Half-past-three on the dot.
I lie there, sigh there, in the watches of the night,
Awakened by who knows what.

Was I startled up by trouble in an anxious dream,
Or by a distant clunk on the road?
Perhaps some mischief of the cat, or a change
In shift among the crickets and the toads?

Perhaps I was a monk in some distant life,
In the habit of chanting the Vespers;
Or could it be the rustling of the prairie wind
As through the trees he whispers?

I lie in the darkness, on the borderlands of sleep,
Restless, alone, and lonely,
Chided by the whispering of my familiar demons—
Should-Have, What-If, If-Only.

I want to sleep, but my mind's a whirl of words.
In vain I try to fight them;
But the opening lines of this poem come to me,
So I must get up and write them.

ALPHABETICAL INDEX

ALPHABETICAL INDEX

ALPHABETICAL INDEX

ALPHABETICAL INDEX

TOPICAL INDEX

Songs of Christmastide

Songs of the Seasons

TOPICAL INDEX

Songs of Love

Songs of Nature

TOPICAL INDEX

Songs of Light

Songs of Night

TOPICAL INDEX

Songs of Inspiration

TOPICAL INDEX

Songs of Faith

TOPICAL INDEX

Songs of Times Long Passed

Songs of a Life Well Lived

TOPICAL INDEX

Songs of Quiet Reflection

TOPICAL INDEX

Songs of Bitterness

TOPICAL INDEX

Songs for Our Troubled Times

Songs of Collective Identity

TOPICAL INDEX

ACKNOWLEDGEMENTS

· ————◄●►———— ·

There are many wonderful people whom I should like to thank for the poems in this book.

I thank my family, for putting up with my eccentricities.

I thank the composers who entrusted their voices to me, and especially to my brother, Eric Whitacre, without whose support and friendship I would never have begun this journey.

I thank the wonderful people at Walton and GIA for their generosity and confidence, most especially Susan LaBarr and Alec Harris, for believing in me and making this happen.

I thank the many directors who have commissioned me, and programmed my words and brought them to so many amazing spaces around the world.

I thank the host of singers who have given life to these words, and who will continue to do so long after I am gone. It is an indescribable feeling to hear one's heart so boldly sung out in the voices of others.

Finally, to my Julie, who in many ways is still on this journey with me, inspiring me and rooting for me from the other side of eternity. Built into the DNA of these poems are my joy, my loss, my grief, my healing, and my hope.

And many thanks and rich blessings to you.

CHORAL EDITION
PUBLISHER INFORMATION

The following poems were written for choral works published by the listed publishers.

Across the Sea (Over Havet) – Hinshaw Music
Across the Vast, Eternal Sky – Walton Music
A Bronze Triptych – Hinshaw Music
The Chelsea Carol – Shadow Water Music
A Christmas Lullaby – Hinshaw Music
Dreamweaver – Walton Music
Heaven Unfolding – Boosey & Hawkes
Her Sacred Spirit Soars – Shadow Water Music
Himenami (The Divine Wave) – Hinshaw Music
I Am – G. Schirmer, Inc.
Leonardo Dreams of His Flying Machine – Walton Music
Light, Love – Schott Music
Luminous Night of the Soul – Walton Music
Lux Aurumque – Walton Music
Nox Aurumque – Shadow Water Music
Oread Farewell – Hinshaw Music
Over Havet – Hinshaw Music
River's Lament – Boosey & Hawkes
Sainte-Chapelle – Shadow Water Music
Seasons – Walton Music
Sleep – Walton Music
Stars in Heaven – Faber Music
Stella Clara – Hinshaw Music
Then, and Still – Walton Music
Tonight I Dance Alone – Bärenreiter Verlag
Tundra – Walton Music
#twitterlieder – ECS Publishing
Virgo, Mater, Regina – Walton Music
Voces Lucis – Santa Barbara Music Publishing
Wintertide – Walton Music

Lyricist, author, and composer Charles Anthony Silvestri has worked with leading artists from all over the world to create texts tailor-made for their commissions and specific artistic needs. He enjoys the challenge of solving these creative problems and has provided custom choral texts, opera libretti, program notes, and other writing for composers, including Eric Whitacre, Ola Gjeilo, and Dan Forrest, and for groups ranging from high schools to the Houston Grand Opera, from the King's Singers to the San Francisco Gay Men's Chorus, from Westminster Choir College to Westminster Abbey.

As a clinician, Silvestri speaks to choirs, classes, and concert audiences about his works, the creative process, the marriage of words and music, and about his collaborative relationships with composers.

He lives with his children in Lawrence, Kansas. For more on Silvestri's work, see www.charlesanthonysilvestri.com.